The
Road
to
Reward

Living Today in Light of Tomorrow

The
Road
to
Reward

Living Today in Light of Tomorrow

Robert N. Wilkin

Grace Evangelical Society

Irving, Texas

The Road to Reward: Living Today in Light of Tomorrow
Copyright © 2003 by Grace Evangelical Society
Printed in the United States of America

Unless otherwise noted, Scripture citations are from *The New King James Version,* Copyright © 1979, 1980, 1982, by Thomas Nelson, Inc.

Cover and book design: Michael Makidon
Production: Cathy Beach

Library of Congress Cataloging-in-Publication Data
Wilkin, Robert N., 1952-
The road to reward: living today in light of tomorrow / Robert N. Wilkin
Includes bibliographical references.
ISBN 0-9641392-6-X
1. Rewards. 2. Salvation. 3. Christian Life.

Requests for information should be addressed to:
Grace Evangelical Society
PO Box 155018
Irving, TX 75015-5018

Phone: 972.257.1160
Web: http://www.faithalone.org

*This book is lovingly dedicated
to the many partners in grace
whose support has made it possible.
Thank you for your faithfulness.
Together we are promoting
the wonderful messages
of the free gift of eternal life
and the costly prize of eternal reward.
Sola fide.*

— TABLE OF CONTENTS —

~ Section 1 ~

Is Eternal Salvation a Reward?

*Now to him who works,
the wages are not counted as grace but as debt.
But to him who does not work
but believes on Him who justifies the ungodly,
his faith is accounted for righteousness.*
Romans 4:4-5

— Chapter 1 —

THE DISASTER OF
POOR COMMUNICATION

On July 28, 1945, the heavy cruiser *Indianapolis* left Guam for Leyte Gulf, in the Philippine Islands. She radioed the standard message to Leyte that she was on her way, but due to atmospheric interference the signal was scrambled, and Leyte received nothing intelligible.

This lack of communication proved disastrous, for at 12:15 a.m. on July 29, the *Indianapolis* was hit by two torpedoes from a Japanese submarine, the first one knocking out the electrical system, preventing an SOS call. She sank in twelve minutes. Nine hundred of the 1,200 men aboard survived the sinking, taking refuge in the few lifeboats afloat or clinging to debris, hoping for a quick rescue. However, since no one knew when the ship was expected in port, the sailors waited in vain. Over three days passed before search planes finally spotted the survivors—only 316 of the original 900 were still alive. It was a tragic loss caused by poor communication.[1]

I understand the disaster of poor communication. As a young boy, I joined a religious group that taught that eternal life was something you earned—something that came to you only after a good deal of personal sacrifice and holy living. An offshoot of a Holiness church, this group was incredibly extreme in its views and convinced me that if I didn't get my life cleaned up enough, I might miss even the *opportunity* to be saved. However, they did assure me that if I succeeded in cleaning my life up before my window of opportunity came (a period of one to two weeks that could occur anytime between the ages of five and twenty), then salvation was mine. Now as depressing as that was—it got worse. They also taught that once I had obtained eternal life, I would lose it if I committed *even one sin*—with no chance of ever getting it back.

My experience in that religious group influenced me in more ways than one. Early on, it made me very *resistant* to the grace of God. However, once God broke through my resistance, my background actually compelled me to become a strong *advocate* for the grace of God and the freeness of eternal life.

Now I realize that it might seem strange to start a book on eternal rewards by talking about eternal life; however, there's good reason to begin here. You see, many people in our world think just as I did—that eternal life *is* our reward. As a teenager, eternal life was something I was fervently striving to gain and keep. It *was* the eternal reward I sought. But this was only another example of the disaster of poor communication.

— Eternal Life Is Free —

In contrast to the message I heard as a young man, the Lord Jesus spoke of eternal life, not as a *reward*, but as "the *gift* of God" (John 4:10, emphasis mine). Jesus made a simple yet profound promise: "He who believes in Me has everlasting life" (John 6:47). We can take Him at His word. He is not trying to trick us. The Lord Jesus guarantees eternal life to all who simply believe in Him for it (compare 1 Timothy 1:16). It really is that simple! And once we believe in Him, we can begin to obey Him in the matter of laying up treasure in heaven.

Whenever justification salvation is presented as a reward, there are at least three negative side effects.

First, if we lose this distinction, we also lose assurance. We can't be sure we are born again unless we know that eternal life is a gift that is received simply by faith in Jesus Christ. Only the biblical gospel unmixed with rewards theology allows the Christian to remain sure that he has everlasting life.

Second, we cannot evangelize clearly if we fail to recognize this difference. How can we help someone else find assurance if we are not sure ourselves? If we are wondering whether we have done enough to get into heaven, then we can't possibly share the good news clearly with others.

Third, once this distinction is abandoned, our motivation to live for Christ becomes distorted. Instead of being motivated out of love, gratitude, and a desire for reward, we are motivated by fear of hell. Legalism is the offspring of insecurity. When eternal life *is* the reward, we cease to be properly motivated to live for God.

— When You Doubt —

It's clear from Scripture that God doesn't want you to be in doubt about your eternal destiny. He wants you to *know* that you have eternal life (1 John 5:13). So if you lack assurance, why not ask God to show you the truth and to make His Word understandable to you?

Also, I suggest that you read the Gospel of John through several times, praying for God to open your eyes. Take the time to highlight all of the promises God makes to those who simply believe in Christ for eternal life. The promises of God are the key to finding assurance of salvation. We are not saved through the promises *we* make to God but through the promises *He* makes to us! You can rest your eternal destiny confidently on this promise from the Gospel of John. Jesus said:

> *For God so loved the world that He gave His only begotten Son, that whoever believes in Him should not perish but have everlasting life.*
> —John 3:16

You can take Christ at His word—*whoever* believes in Him for everlasting life has it! He has never broken a single promise He has ever made. He never will.

— Conclusion —

As we begin a consideration of eternal rewards, I don't want to be guilty of poor communication: *eternal life is absolutely free, but eternal rewards are not.* John 6:47 and many other passages make it clear that the only thing God requires of us for eternal life is faith in His immutable promise. This is important because, when we lose sight of this fact, all the rewards passages of the New Testament suddenly become a list of instructions for what we must do to obtain and keep eternal life. And when people view rewards passages this way, assurance is lost and along with it, the most powerful motivation for serving God found in the Bible—gratitude for His "indescribable gift" (2 Corinthians 9:15).

---

[1] Virgil Hurley, *Speaker's Sourcebook of New Illustrations* (Dallas, TX: Word Publishing, 2000), 91.

— Chapter 2 —

WAGES AREN'T GIFTS

University professors in England went on a one-day strike in the spring of 1999 to protest their salaries. The Association of University Teachers was seeking a ten percent pay raise and subsequently rejected an offer of a 3.5 percent increase.

In the summer of 2000, teachers in Australia sought a thirty percent pay raise. Later that year Air Afrique pilots went on a one-day strike over their salaries.

NFL referees rejected an offer in 2001 that would have given them an immediate forty percent pay increase and doubled their pay within two years.

Everyone wants to earn a fair wage—hence the rise of unions and strikes and salary negotiations. Indeed, God's Word indicates that we should receive fair wages: "The laborer is worthy of his wages" (Luke 10:7; 1 Timothy 5:18).

Wouldn't it be fantastic to know that for the rest of your life no employer would underpay you? You would receive completely fair compensation for the work you did. Sure, that would be great. We all want to get our fair share from our labors.

As important as our salaries are, they are of little significance compared to what we will receive from the Lord Jesus in eternity for serving Him in this life. There will be no need to negotiate our eternal compensation for serving Christ now. The Lord promises to give us what is fair.

We work for pay in our jobs here and now. But to many Christians the idea of working for the Lord Jesus for pay is a completely foreign concept. To them, serving Jesus is something they should do because they love Him, because it is their duty, because they want to please Him, and because they know life goes better when they live it God's way.

While all of those are admirable motivations for service, it is vital that every Christian knows that when he is serving Christ, he is working for wages.

— Rewarded for Works —

The Greek word translated "rewards" is *misthos*. When a day laborer worked a twelve-hour day, he was paid his wages, or *misthos*. See Matthew 20:1-16.

There are twenty-nine New Testament occurrences of *misthos*.[1] As you study these, you will see that rewards are something more than the gift of eternal life believers receive at the moment of faith.

They are not, however, the only passages dealing with the doctrine. Many other texts allude to the concept without using the word *misthos*. Other key rewards words and phrases you will encounter are "approval" (*dokimos*), "disapproval" (*adokimos*), "ruling with Christ," "inheriting the kingdom," "reaping everlasting life," "blamelessness," "being confessed by Christ," "boldness or shame at His coming," "the Judgment Seat [Bema] of Christ," and "Jesus as Judge."

— Justified by Faith —

As I stated in the previous chapter, many people have the idea that entering the kingdom is a reward. They figure that if they make it, then they have all the reward that anyone could want. Yet look at Paul's words in Romans 4:4-5:

> *Now to him who works, the wages [misthos] are not counted as grace but as debt. But to him who does not work but believes on Him who justifies the ungodly, his faith is accounted for righteousness.*

Notice how the doctrine of rewards must be understood in order to maintain the doctrine of justification by faith alone. The person who thinks that he must do good works to stay saved, or to prove he is saved, does not believe that God *justifies the ungodly*. Nor does he believe that *his faith is accounted for righteousness*. Jesus guarantees eternal life to all who simply believe in Him (John 11:25-27).

We must keep the distinction between wages and grace. Otherwise we obscure assurance and the good news. And we cannot hope to accurately witness to others if we mistakenly think that justification is a reward.

— Distinct and Separate —

When you get your paycheck, you don't thank your employer for the gift, do you? Most likely you think, "I'm grateful to have a job I enjoy that pays me a livable wage. I earned this and I can put it to good use."

Now let's say you were in serious financial need and a person at your church simply gave you $1,000 so that you could make your mortgage payment and avoid losing your house. Would you think, "Wow, it's great that I earned this money"? No. Most likely you would say, "Thank the Lord for such a wonderful and thoughtful gift. I don't deserve it, but I really appreciate it."

Make no mistake here. Eternal life is a gift.[2] Rewards are not. We must keep these two distinct.

In this life we receive our wages once or twice a month. God pays us in this life in many ways as well—and more than once or twice a month. He gives us the fruit of the Spirit. He provides us with food to eat, clothes to wear, and a place to stay. But our ultimate payday will occur after this life is over when we as believers will appear at the Judgment Seat of Christ.

Are you living today in light of *that* day? By focusing on your eternal payday you will glorify God more now, and you will store up greater wages for eternity.

---

[1] There are ten occurrences in Matthew (5:12, 46; 6:1, 2, 5, 16; 10:41 (twice), 42; 20:8); six in Paul (Romans 4:4; 1 Corinthians 3:8, 14; 9:17, 18; 1 Timothy 5:18); four in Luke (Luke 6:23, 35; 10:7; Acts 1:18); four in

John (John 4:36; 2 John 8; Revelation 11:18; 22:12); two in Peter (2 Peter 2:13, 15); and one each in Mark (9:41), James (5:4), and Jude (11).

² More precisely, *the present reception of eternal life in Jesus* is a gift. There are passages (see Chapter 3, for example), in which *a potential future gaining of eternal life* is clearly a reward. There, however, mere life is not in view. Abundance of eternal life is a reward.

— Chapter 3 —

WE REALLY DO REAP WHAT WE SOW

Galatians 6:6-10

It was the illustrious, steel-faced coach of the Dallas Cowboys, Tom Landry, who said:

> I've seen the difference character makes in individual football players. Give me a choice between an outstanding athlete with poor character and a lesser athlete of good character, and I'll choose the latter every time. The athlete with good character will often perform to his fullest potential and be a successful football player, while the outstanding athlete with poor character will usually fail to play up to his potential and often won't even achieve average performance.[1]

The key factor in productivity is not ability. It's character that counts. This principle holds true in our Christian lives as well. Only the believer who is humble and continually seeking God's glory will reach his or her potential in life.

All believers have the potential of experiencing the life God has given them in an abundant way. But as we shall see in Galatians 6:6-10, some fail to live up to their potential. They indulge the flesh, grow tired while doing good, and lose heart. And when that occurs, these believers suffer great loss.

The loss they incur answers one of the greatest objections people have to the doctrine of justification by faith alone—that it seems to promote sin. "If I believed that, why wouldn't I go out and live like the devil?" is a question I've heard many times while explaining the good news to people. They have difficulty understanding why a person who knew he was secure eternally would choose to live for God.

Actually, there are a number of compelling reasons for an eternally secure believer to choose to live a godly life. Paul powerfully states one of them in Galatians 6:7:

> *Do not be deceived, God is not mocked; for whatever a man sows, that he will also reap.*

The problem, as I see it, is that most people simply do not believe this. They rationalize that if those who merely believe in Christ are eternally secure, then they are also free to sin with impunity.

But in reality, the only way anyone can expect to find peace, joy, and contentment is by living life the way God directs. The principle of sowing and reaping applies to all people, including believers.

— God Is Not Mocked —

The idea that eternally secure people have no reason to live for God inadvertently demonstrates a very low opinion of God, giving the impression that God is powerless to motivate His children to obey Him.

Earthly parents have no ability to threaten their children with hell. Yet good parents are able to motivate their children to obey them. The American government can't send anyone to hell either, but it has many ways of motivating obedience to its laws. Is God less powerful than earthly parents or human government? No one—believer or unbeliever—can live like the devil and "get away with it." That would be mocking God!

On one occasion the prophet Elisha was being mocked by a group of teenage hooligans. His mentor, the prophet Elijah, had just gone up to heaven alive in a whirlwind. Now the youths shouted to Elisha, "Go up, baldhead."

God doesn't often respond to mocking with instant capital punishment, but He did that day. He had Elisha pronounce a curse on the youths. Two bears came out of the woods and mauled forty-two of them to death. God is not mocked with impunity. Sometimes the judgment is immediate. Sometimes it comes later. But it always comes (see 2 Kings 2:23-25).

In Galatians 6:6-10, Paul is not focusing on judgment here and now. The emphasis, as we shall see, is on future judgment at the Judgment Seat of Christ. However, the principle that God is not mocked has application both now and forever. The believer who departs to the proverbial spiritual far country (Luke 15:13) will experience judgment now and then again at the Bema.

— Not Free-Gift Language —

Galatians 6:6-10 is not a passage about justification by faith alone. Eternal salvation is a free gift (John 4:10; Ephesians 2:8-9; Romans 4:4-5) received by faith alone in Christ alone (John 6:35-40; 11:25-27). And it is a present possession (John 5:24; 6:47).

Therefore, whatever "reaping eternal life" means, it can't contradict other Scripture. What else but eternal rewards could be in view, since those indeed are earned and are future? If Paul were speaking of justification truth, then he, like the Lord Jesus, would refer to having eternal life right now. "He who believes in Me *has* everlasting life" (John 6:47, emphasis mine) is far different from "He who sows to the Spirit *will* of the Spirit *reap* everlasting life" (Galatians 6:8, emphasis mine). The latter passage is neither free-gift language nor present-possession truth.

It is important to keep in mind that whenever eternal life is spoken of as a possible future possession, eternal *rewards* are in view. Whenever eternal life is spoken of as a present possession, then eternal *salvation* is in focus.

— Calling *Believers* to Do Good Works —

That Paul is not talking about justification by faith in Christ is also supported by his emphasis on works and the absence of any mention of faith. The words "believe" and "faith" occur only once in this passage, and then merely as a reference to the fact that we are to make special effort to help our fellow believers "who are of the household of *faith*" (verse 10). Compare this to Galatians 3:6-14 where those words occur ten times to show that the sole condition of justification is faith in Christ.

This paragraph in Galatians 6 begins and ends with calls to do good works. In the first verse of the paragraph (verse 6), there is a call to help those who teach the Bible. "Let him who is taught the word share in all good things with him who teaches." This surely includes financial assistance.

The last two verses in the paragraph (verses 9-10) refer to *doing good.*

> *And let us not grow weary while* doing good, *for in due season we shall reap if we do not lose heart. Therefore, as we have opportunity, let us* do good *to all, especially to those who are of the household of faith.*

The intervening material (verses 7-8) is also about doing good. We are not to sow to the flesh; rather, we are to sow to the Spirit.

Of course, I realize many well-intentioned people believe that Paul is warning professing believers that if they fail to persevere in good works they will go to hell, since they will have proved to be false professors. Such thinking, however, destroys the freeness of the gospel, eliminates the doctrine of eternal rewards, and, is directly contradicted by the context.

Paul makes it crystal clear that believers should fear losing heart and failing to reap everlasting life. So doesn't this mean that believers can lose eternal salvation? No. As we shall soon see, Paul uses the expression "eternal life" here to refer to fullness of life forever.

Before we consider the meaning of eternal life in this passage, it is vital that we observe that Paul's use of the first person plural in verse 9 includes himself. If *we* lose heart, *we* will not reap eternal life. On another occasion (1 Corinthians 9:24-27) he even used the first person singular (compare 2 Timothy 2:12 and 4:7-8). Paul was not sure that he would persevere and gain *the full experience of eternal life* that goes to those who endure. Yet Paul knew with certainty that he was eternally secure (Galatians 2:15-16; 3:6-14; 2 Timothy 1:12).

— A Life Full of Potential —

The expression "eternal life" in the New Testament is used in two different senses. Often it refers to spiritual life that never ends. For example, the Lord Jesus promised that "whoever lives and believes in Me shall never die" (John 11:26).

However, eternal life does not merely refer to unending life. Since eternal life is God's kind of life (Jesus said, "I am the life"), it is a life full of creative potential. As such, it is a life that can be experienced to greater or lesser degrees. Just as there is great range in the way unbelievers utilize their lives, so there is with believers as well.

The Lord Jesus Himself is called "eternal life" by the apostle John, "And we are in Him who is true, in His Son Jesus Christ. This is the true God and eternal life" (1 John 5:20). The Lord Jesus did not receive life from anyone. To quote John again, "In Him was life" (John 1:4). Because of this, Jesus could say something that no one else could, "I lay down My life that I may take it again...I have power to lay it down, and I have power to take it again" (John 10:17-18). When Jesus rose from the dead, *He raised Himself up*. "Destroy this temple, and in three days I will raise it up" (John 2:19).

Our God-given life is full of potential. A new Christian does not experience the quality of eternal life that a mature believer does. As a person grows in Christ, so does his experience of eternal life. We all know senior saints who are marvelous examples of this. They are experiencing the abundant life of which Jesus spoke, "I have come that they may have life, and that they may have it more abundantly" (John 10:10b). As Jody Dillow noted:

> Eternal life is no static entity but a relationship with God. It is dynamic and growing and has degrees. Some Christians have a more intimate relationship with God than others. They have a richer experience of eternal life.[2]

Galatians 6:8 is the only place in the Bible where we find the expression "reaping eternal life." However, there are similar expressions in Matthew 19:29 ("inherit everlasting life") and in Luke 18:30 ("receive...in the age to come everlasting life"). In all three of these passages reaping, inheriting, and receiving eternal life refer to having a *fuller experience of His life* in the future.[3]

— Let Us Not Grow Weary —

Once we receive the gift of eternal life, the *fact* of our eternal *existence* as children of God is secure. However, the *quality* of our eternal *experience* is not secure until we die. All believers will have joy forever, but only some will have *abundant* joy forever. How we live our Christian lives will determine what we reap in the life to come.

God conditions this future harvest upon works. The analogy of sowing and reaping is taken from farming. It takes a lot of effort to plow the ground, sow the seeds, water, weed, and then harvest. Only by persistent hard work will a farmer reap a good crop. So, too, only by persistent hard work will the believer reap an abundant eternal experience (see also 1 Corinthians 9:24-27 and 2 Timothy 2:6).

The quality of life varies greatly among people. Money and possessions are not the decisive factors. We all know of wealthy people whose lives are empty and without direction. And we know others with fewer financial resources whose lives are full and meaningful. What determines quality of life is attitude. In eternity all believers will have significance and direction. Yet some will experience life more fully and serve God to a greater degree.

Galatians 6:9 is a powerful reminder to the believer: "Let us not grow weary while doing good, for in due season we shall reap if we do not lose heart." It's not enough to begin well. Even hanging in there in our service for Christ for decades is not enough. In order to reap, we must endure to the end.

At the 1984 Summer Olympics in Los Angeles, the first women's Olympic marathon was held. One scene from that race stands out above all the rest. The scene to which I refer is not Joan Benoit Samuelson crossing the finish line first. It isn't about someone who won a medal, but about an also-ran.

Gabrielle Andersen-Scheiss, a Swiss-American runner, became ill during the race.[4] By the twenty-four-mile mark she was reduced to an awkward jog. By twenty-five miles she could barely walk. Yet she kept on, determined to finish, even though the race for the medals was long over.

Somehow she made it into the stadium—one lap to go. The TV monitors captured her image. Hundreds of millions of people were aghast. Gabrielle was staggering from one side of the track to the other. Four times in the final lap officials approached her urging her to quit. Four times she awkwardly waved them off. Stumbling across the finish line, she collapsed.[5]

It still brings tears to my eyes when I think of what she did that day. Oh, how I want to finish the Christian life well, in spite of the problems and difficulties ahead!

— Conclusion —

The reception of eternal life at the point of initial faith in Christ is just the beginning of the Christian life. From that point forward believers have the opportunity to lay up eternal rewards. We are in the process now of determining the quality of our eternal experience. Make no mistake—effort is involved in order to have a full experience of eternal life now and forever.

While all believers will live in the kingdom, only believers who persist in good works will enjoy a special abundance of life.

All of us are repeatedly tempted to throw in the spiritual towel. The flesh wars against the Spirit and won't quit until we go to be with the Lord (Galatians 5:17). A desire for abundant eternal life should be one motivating factor to keep on keeping on in the Christian life.

Don't give up. Our judgment day, the Judgment Seat of Christ, is coming. A lot is at stake. The quality of our eternal experience hangs in the balance.

---

[1] Edythe Draper, *Draper's Book of Quotations for the Christian World* (Wheaton: Tyndale House Publishers, Inc., 1992). Entries 1017-1019.

[2] Joseph C. Dillow, *The Reign of the Servant Kings: A Study of Eternal Security and the Final Significance of Man* (Hayesville, NC: Schoettle Publishing Company, 1992), 140.

[3] See Dillow, 140. He says, "In every place where eternal life is presented as something which can be obtained by works, it is contextually **always** described as a future acquisition. Conversely, whenever eternal life is described as something in the present, it is obtained by faith alone."

[4] For a picture of her from the race and a brief account, see http://www.olympic.org/uk/games/past/facts_uk.asp?OLGT=1&OLGY=1984.

[5] The story has a happy ending: Gabrielle recovered fully after the race.

~ Section 2 ~

WHO RECEIVES REWARDS?

Well done, good servant;
because you were faithful in a very little,
have authority over ten cities.
Luke 19:17

— Chapter 4 —

FAITHFUL SERVANTS
Luke 19:11-27

S tacy Dragila, winner of the gold medal in the 2000 Olympics in Sydney, Australia, is the greatest women's pole-vaulter of all time.[1] She holds both the indoor and outdoor world records. Eight times in 2001, she set new world records.

In August of 2001 Stacy competed in the International Track and Field Championships in Edmonton, Alberta. She had a good opportunity to win the World Championships, but at no point could she afford to give a half hearted effort. Perseverance is one of the hallmarks of any great athlete. So it is for anyone who wishes to be great in God's service.

— Setting the Stage —

In the Parable of the Minas found in Luke 19:11-27, the Lord indicates that He is going away (in His death, resurrection, and ascension), leaving His servants with work to do, and then returning to evaluate how each one did. Each of the servants are given one mina, a sum of money equivalent to about $10,000 today. While we know that not all people have the same degree of ability in life, this parable is answering a key question: If three people have equal ability and opportunity, yet they have a wide range of productivity in their service for Christ, how will He evaluate and recompense their varied service?

Let's see how each servant fares in this judgment.

— The All-Star —

The first person in the parable clearly performed best, multiplying the money the Lord gave him ten times (Luke 19:16). This man maximized his abilities and opportunities.

Surely this is meant to illustrate the believer who serves Christ wholeheartedly throughout his Christian life. Though he wasn't perfect, he gave the Lord his best efforts. His heart was in the right place and he was laying up treasures in heaven, not on earth (Matthew 6:19-21).

The Lord's response to this all-star believer was, "Well done, good servant; because you were faithful in a very little, have authority over ten cities" (Luke 19:17). First, this servant heard, "Well done, good servant." What great words to hear from the King of kings!

Second, he learned about a tangible reward he would receive for his good service. "Have authority over ten cities." Clearly Jesus was speaking of His eternal kingdom here. This type of servant would reign over "ten cities."

Make no mistake. This person was not being told that he would get into the kingdom. Rather, he was being informed about the ministry he would receive when he got there. In the age to come, only the most faithful servants from this life will have major authority in the kingdom.

We should not overlook the fact that this is a grand promotion. The Lord said, "Because you were faithful *in a very little…*" There are many ways we can faithfully serve Christ in this life. The All-Star might be one who serves faithfully for fifty years as an elder in a small rural church. Or it might be a missionary couple who serve in a hostile culture for decades, while seeing very few come to faith in Christ. It might be a widow who had been a wonderful wife and mother and who remains a mainstay in her local church. But whatever ministry he or she has in this life is called "very little" by the Lord in comparison to the ministry that lies ahead.

— The Journeyman —

In every sport there are professional athletes called journeymen. They play their sport faithfully for many years, yet without distinction. Such people may or may not maximize their talents.

Ryan Leaf appears to be a journeyman quarterback. He was the second player taken in the 1998 draft. He is 6 foot 5, weighs 235, and has a cannon for an arm. Yet in his three years in San Diego, he won very few games. Still, Ryan Leaf has accomplished something. He completed 272 passes, 13 for touchdowns. He personally ran the ball 55 times. He played in pain, and also under a lot of criticism.

In the 2001 season he was signed by the Cowboys for the veteran minimum of $500,000, even though it was discovered he had a major problem in his throwing wrist. Why? Because the Cowboys needed additional quarterbacks, and Ryan Leaf had something to contribute. Even a person who fails to reach his full potential is rewarded for what he does.

The second servant in the parable is somewhat like a journeyman who fails to maximize his talents. He had the same amount of ability and opportunity as the first servant, as is represented by the one mina with which they each started. But the second servant failed to contribute as much as he could have. "Master, your mina has earned five minas" (Luke 19:18). Not a great return.

While the Lord had no words of praise for him, what He did say was still encouraging: "You also be over five cities" (Luke 19:19). That is a far cry from the praise and authority the first servant received. Yet this second servant would rule with Christ in His kingdom. Five minas resulted in five cities.

Now there are many different ways in which believers might achieve only half of what the Lord has for them to accomplish. Some might serve Him halfheartedly for their entire Christian lives. Others might serve Him wholeheartedly for half of their Christian lives. Still others might run hot and cold again and again.

— The Scared Shirker —

While many suggest that the third servant is an unfaithful unbeliever, the evidence overwhelmingly shows that this servant is an unfaithful *believer*.[2] First, this person is a servant of Christ. Unbelievers are not. Second, he is entrusted with something to invest for his Lord. Unbelievers are not. Third, he is neither rebuked for lack of faith, nor told that the Lord never knew him. Unbelievers are (compare Matthew 7:21-23). Fourth, he is clearly contrasted with unbelievers. Immediately after his judgment we read these words, "But bring here those enemies of mine, who did not want me to reign over them [i.e., didn't want to be in a kingdom with this person as their king], and slay them before me" (verse 27). The word "but" unequivocally indicates that the third servant was not part of the group that is slain. Slaying here is figurative for eternal separation from the kingdom.

I call the third servant a "scared shirker" because of what he did and how he justified it. He didn't do as the other two servants did, and invest the money in ventures that generated good returns. He didn't even put it in the bank where at least it could have earned some interest. He just hid it.[3]

Here is what he said in his defense:

> *Master, here is your mina, which I have kept put away in a handkerchief. For I feared you, because you are an austere man. You collect what you did not deposit, and reap what you did not sow.*
> —Luke 19:20-21

What he is saying is that he feared doing something wrong and losing the mina altogether. He knew that the Lord was holding him accountable and wanted a return on the money He had given him.

Bishop W. C. Magee once said, "The man who makes no mistakes usually does not make anything." It is true that if you don't take any risks in life, you probably won't have any big losses. But you also won't accomplish much.

If the third servant was so concerned about pleasing his master, why didn't he put the money in the bank to earn at least a small return?

We mustn't conclude that this type of person never did even one good work. Surely only believers who die at the moment of regeneration will do absolutely no good works. It merely means the person failed to come up with even a minimal return on investment.

What is the return in view? In many other places in Scripture, ruling with Christ is conditioned upon ongoing confession of Christ (e.g., 2 Timothy 2:12; Hebrews 10:23). A person may do good works, yet without confessing his faith in Christ. Thus the minimal return required is persevering in open confession of our faith in Christ.

There are many ways in which we may confess our faith in Christ. Evangelism is one way. Telling others we are Christians, which is really pre-evangelism, is another. Going to church and serving there are other ways in which we identify ourselves as believers (Hebrews 10:23-25). Baptism is certainly a public testimony of our faith (Matthew 28:18-20). And when we disciple other believers, we are professing our faith in Christ to them, and to anyone who knows we are teaching others about Christ.

In a sense, any ministry we do in and through the local church is professing Christ. To be at least a Journeyman, we must make our faith in Christ public. However, to be an All-Star, we need to do more than simply show others that we are Christians. We must *maximize* our time, talent, and treasure for Christ. Half-hearted service will not result in the commendation, "Well done, good servant."

The minas represent the time, talent, and treasure God has given us to serve Him by ministering to others in His name. It is thus fitting that for each mina earned, the servant gains authority over another city in the life to come. Our level of authority in the coming life will be directly related to our ministry to people in this life.

— Pursuing the Prize —

Stacy Dragila won the gold medal in the 2001 World Championships. Interestingly, the second place competitor actually cleared the same height. Stacy won because she had fewer misses at lower heights. Her persistence in training paid off.

When athletes look back on their careers, all they can hope for is to have done the best with their God-given abilities. The same is true of the Christian. Our aim should be to have His full approval when we reach the end of our lives. We should want to maximize our lives for Christ so that we will hear those blessed words, "Well done, good servant." Oh, to hear those words from the One who means so much to us.

---

[1] For more information on Stacy and her vaulting, see http://www.huddlin.com/_huddle/index.html.

[2] See Zane C. Hodges, *The Gospel Under Siege*, revised and enlarged edition (Dallas: Redención Viva, 1981, 1992), 130-32 and Joseph C. Dillow, *The Reign of the Servant Kings: A Study of Eternal Security and the Final Significance of Man* (Hayesville, NC: Schoettle Publishing Company, 1992), 564-65, 589.

[3] Hiding the money would thus represent failure to confess Christ. This person would be a secret believer like Nicodemus in the Gospel of John. Sadly there are some believers today who think that they don't need to go to church or be baptized or tell others about their faith. They figure their faith is a personal matter. Unfortunately, they are burying that which God expects them to invest in His service.

The Lord said that at the very least this servant should have invested the money He gave him in the bank. What does that represent? Well, this servant failed to confess Christ. Thus the very least he could have done would have been to give the money so that others could do what he would not—evangelize and disciple.

— Chapter 5 —

LOVING DISCIPLES
1 John 2:28; 4:17-19

Many Christians don't realize that they may feel shame when they stand before Christ at His Judgment Seat. Yet, we will have confidence before Him at His coming only if we abide in Him. The believer who makes himself at home with the world and not with Christ, will be ashamed of himself on that day:

> *And now, little children, abide in Him, that when He appears, we may have confidence and not be ashamed before Him at His coming.*
> —1 John 2:28

In his commentary on the Johannine epistles, Zane Hodges discusses confidence and shame at the Bema:

> Even though eternal salvation is an entirely free gift which can never be lost, the New Testament makes plain that the believer must give an account of his or her Christian life in the presence of Christ (cf. 2 Corinthians 5:10; Romans 14:10-12)... Therefore, shame is decidedly possible at

the Judgment Seat. This is all the more true since Christians at that time will have their eternal bodies. Thus sin will no longer inhibit appropriate regret and embarrassment about those things in one's earthly life that did not please the Lord.[1]

Instead of shame, the apostle John suggests that his readers can have *confidence...before Him at His coming.* "Confidence" translates a Greek word (*parrēsia*) that may also mean "boldness" or "fearlessness." Such an experience in the presence of our Lord at His review of our lives is earnestly to be desired.

Some believers live as though they couldn't possibly experience shame before Christ. After all, sins are supposed to be forgiven, right?

It is true, of course, that the Lord Jesus by His death on the cross took away all of our sins, past, present, and future (John 1:29; 1 John 2:2). Sin is no longer a barrier to anyone having eternal salvation. The moment we believe in Jesus for eternal life, He gives it to us. Eternal life, however, does not exclude accountability. Believers still need fellowship forgiveness (1 John 1:9). And if a believer is out of fellowship with God when his life is over, he will experience shame at the Bema.

— Fear Is Sometimes Appropriate —

My mother-in-law, Camille, panics every time she sees a police car on the highway. I don't normally share her fear, unless I am doing something wrong!

The same principle applies in relationships. A child raised in a good home need not fear rebuke if he is doing what his parents ask. A student in school who is obeying the teacher's rules need not fear detention. A hardworking employee who is abiding by the office regulations has no reason to fear being put on probation.

The knowledge that actions have consequences motivates us to do right. Many Christians don't stop to think that the same is true in our relationship with God. If we are busy doing what He wants us to do, manifesting His love to others, we need not fear discipline now or rebuke at the Judgment Seat of Christ.

One of the most powerful statements by the apostle John is that "perfect love casts out fear" (1 John 4:18). In fact, it is even more powerful when it is properly understood in the context of the Judgment Seat of Christ and the need for love to be perfected in our hearts.

In 1 John 4:17 the apostle writes,

> *Love has been perfected among us in this: that we may have boldness* in the day of judgment; *because as He is, so are we in this world* (emphasis mine).

There is only one *day of judgment* for the Christian. That is the Bema, or the Judgment Seat of Christ.

Christians will never be judged to determine our eternal destiny (John 5:24). That was settled the moment we believed in Christ (John 3:18). Yet we *will* be judged. The purpose of the

Bema is to recompense believers for work done, whether good or bad (2 Corinthians 5:10).

If we miss this simple fact, we get the wrong impression about where this verse is heading.

— Mature Love Leads to Boldness —

What might John mean by "love has been perfected among [or in] us"? Zane Hodges's comments on this verse are helpful:

> God's love is not *perfected* in a Christian whose heart is simply a reservoir in which to receive it, but only in a Christian whose heart furnishes an aqueduct to convey it to others.[2]

The word "boldness" in 1 John 4:17 is the same Greek word (*parrēsia*) that is translated "confidence" in 2:28, the theme verse for the letter. Believers who abide in Christ will have confidence and boldness when He appears; they will not shrink back in shame at Christ's coming.[3]

Here John concludes this theme. Believers in whom God's love has been perfected will have boldness at the Bema. Like obedient children of good parents, we have nothing to fear. We can and should be confident, for our Lord is a Judge who is loving, gracious, and fair. He will commend believers in whom His love has matured.

— Perfect Love Casts Out Fear —

John goes on to say,

> *"There is no fear in love; but perfect love casts out fear, because fear involves torment. But he who fears has not been made perfect in love."*
>
> —1 John 4:18

This is commonly misunderstood as referring to assurance of salvation. It is thought that if I am sure of God's perfect love for me, then I have no fear of eternal condemnation. Yet this verse is about "the day of judgment" at the Bema, which all believers indeed will face. And it concerns our manifesting God's love to others, not about Him manifesting His love toward us.

John's point is that loving Christians need not fear the Bema. However, a believer who is not mature in love should reasonably fear his coming day of judgment before the Lord.

John is calling us to make loving others our aim in life. He made this point forcefully in 1 John 3:16-23. There he says, "Let us not love in word or in tongue [i.e., Let's not just *talk* about love], but in deed and in truth" (3:18). God's love is active in us only if we are giving of our energy and possessions to help others (3:16-17). And the more we love, by abiding in Christ, the better our judgment will be at His Judgment Seat.

When John says, "Perfect love casts out fear, *because fear involves torment*," he is not talking about eternal torment in hell. John is speaking to believers here ("Beloved," 4:1, 7, 11; compare 2:2, 12-14, 26). The words translated "involves torment"

THE ROAD TO REWARD

(*kolasin echei*) would be better translated as "has punishment" or "is punishment." The idea is that fear is itself a form of divine punishment or discipline.[4] God disciplines us so that we will learn and get back on track. If we respond properly to God's discipline, then we will grow and become more loving. That in turn eliminates the fear.

Some Christians experience false guilt. John has a remedy for such people and it's basically this: chill out.

> *If our heart condemns us* [that we are not loving and hence not abiding in the truth of God], *God is greater than our heart, and knows all things. Beloved if our heart does not condemn us, we have confidence toward God.*
> —1 John 3:20-21

The believer who doesn't *feel* confident about the coming judgment at the Bema, but yet who is walking in fellowship with Christ, should realize that God will take into account all of the loving deeds we have done. It is comforting to realize that we may be harder on ourselves than the Lord Jesus will be.

— Gratitude Can Produce Mature Love —

John ends the body of his epistle with these marvelous words, "We love Him because He first loved us" (1 John 4:19). Believe it or not, this is the first time in the epistle that John speaks directly of our love for God.

What moves us to love God? It is His love for us! Gratitude is a powerful motivator.

Mature love develops as we grow to appreciate what God has done for us in Christ. It all starts with Him. Jesus told His disciples, "Without Me you can do nothing" (John 15:5).[5]

I used to think that we could live the Christian life by commitment of the will; that we could please God by trying hard. Then I came to see that what God wants from us is faith in Him. Our lives are transformed only by the renewing of our minds (Romans 12:1-2). And mind renewal starts with loving God. If we don't love God, no amount of commitment can produce godliness. Commitment without love produces legalism.

— Conclusion —

As the apostle John shows, our coming day of judgment should powerfully motivate us to grow and mature in our love for one another.

Mature love casts out fear of the Bema. If you live each day in light of *that* day, God's love will become more mature in you. The people around you will be blessed. God will be glorified. And you will have reason to look toward the Bema with confidence.

---

[1] Zane C. Hodges, *The Epistles of John: Walking in the Light of God's Love* (Irving, TX: Grace Evangelical Society, 2000), 125.

[2] Ibid., 198-99, emphasis his.

[3] There is a play on words here in Greek that is missed in English. The word for Christ's *coming* is *parousia*. It rhymes with the word for boldness, *parrēsia*. John wants us to have *parrēsia* at the *parousia*.

[4] Hodges, *The Epistles of John*, 202.

[5] The idea of abiding in Christ and having mature love is found throughout the Upper Room Discourse (John 13–17). See especially John 14:15 ("If you love Me, keep My commandments") and 15:12-14, 17 ("This is My commandment, that you love one another as I have loved you. Greater love has no one than this, than to lay down one's life for his friends. You are my friends if you do whatever I command you...These things I command you, that you love one another").

— Chapter 6 —

NIKE CHRISTIANS
2 Timothy 2:11-13

The one word that best describes Thomas Alva Edison is *persistent*. Certainly he would never have invented the modern lightbulb and numerous other inventions if he had been one to give up.

The first electric light was actually invented in 1800 by an English scientist, Sir Humphry Davy. By connecting wires to a battery and hooking the wires up to carbon, Davy produced an electric arc.

By 1879 various efforts at making electric lights had been tried in England and America, but no one had come up with a type of filament that would conduct electricity, glow, and yet not burn up quickly. Edison tried hundreds of possible filaments, with failure being the one constant. Before he finally found something that would work, he experienced over 900 failures in a row! But Edison knew that the prize was well worth the effort and the frustration.

Finally he discovered that a carbon filament in an oxygen-free bulb glowed for forty hours before going out. He eventually produced a bulb that could glow for over 1,500 hours.

I grew up in Southern California where the electric company is called Southern California Edison. His name is one of the most recognizable in our world today. He gained prestige, honor, fame, and wealth for himself and his heirs.

His fame was not the result of his birth (his father was a carpenter), his education (his teachers thought he was a poor student), or good luck. Believing that persistent hard work paid off, Edison worked many twenty-hour days. He often said, "Genius is one percent inspiration and ninety-nine percent perspiration."

Because of Edison's unwavering commitment and perseverance, he became one of the most prolific inventors of all time, patenting an amazing 1,093 inventions.

Wouldn't it be great if that same commitment to hard work and perseverance characterized our Christian lives? It can. The recognition that our perseverance pleases God, and will ultimately result in the privilege of ruling with Christ, can motivate such persistence.

— Eternal Life Is Absolutely Secure —

Second Timothy 2:11-13 is a passage that stresses both the freeness of eternal salvation and the costliness of eternal rewards.

> *For if we died with Him,*
> *We shall also live with Him.*
> *If we endure,*
> *We shall also reign with Him.*
> *If we deny Him,*
> *He also will deny us.*

If we are faithless,
He remains faithful;
He cannot deny Himself.

Similar to the four-inch newspaper headlines that proclaimed the end of WW II on VE (Victory in Europe) Day, verses 11 and 13 clearly and forcefully proclaim news of great victory. By virtue of their union with Christ, every Christian is secure forever. It's a done deal that can't be reversed, even by faithlessness on the part of the believer.

Verse 11 says, "If we died with Him, we shall also live with Him." This is another way of saying that every believer has eternal life and can never lose it. If we have believed in Christ for eternal life, then we have died with Him in a positional sense (Romans 6:5, 8; Galatians 2:20; 5:24). By *positional* I mean that God views us as though we died with Jesus on the cross. While in our *experience* we did not die with Christ, God in His grace credits us with having been crucified with Christ.[1]

Three days after He died, the Lord Jesus rose again. Implicit in Paul's statement in verse 11 is the understanding that we who died with Him also rose with Him (see Ephesians 2:6). However, Paul's focus is beyond even our co-resurrection with Christ. His focus is on living with Him forever—"we shall also live with Him."

Just as there is no question that Jesus is eternally secure, so all who died with Him are secure as well. There is no escape clause. There is no such thing as one who has died with Christ but who will fail to live with Him forever.

THE ROAD TO REWARD

As verse 13 says, "If we are faithless, He remains faithful; He cannot deny Himself." Jesus promises eternal life to all who believe in Him. *Our* faithfulness is not part of the equation. It is *His* faithfulness that guarantees that we stay saved. Since He will always be faithful to that which He promised, all believers, including faithless ones, will live with Christ forever.

Paul knew, however, that faithfulness matters to God. Eternal security is not a license to lethargy. Verse 12 reveals the consequences for both *faithfulness* and *faithlessness*. First, Paul considers the consequences for faithfulness.

— Christians Who Endure —

Even a casual reading of the passage shows that verse 12 is discussing something different than verses 11 and 13. While those verses are extremely comforting and encouraging to all believers, verse 12 is comforting and encouraging only to those believers who are currently walking in fellowship with God.

Verse 12a reads, "If we endure, we shall also reign with Him." Paul had spoken of his own endurance, using the same Greek verb, in verse 10. There it clearly refers to persevering in the faith in spite of persecution and suffering (verse 9). If other Christians would follow his example and endure in the faith in spite of persecution and suffering, then they too would rule with Christ.

Some mistakenly think that reigning with Christ is synonymous with being a Christian. However, Paul makes it clear in this passage that while all Christians—including faithless ones—have life, only persevering Christians will rule with Christ.

The Lord Jesus also made it clear that only overcoming Christians will rule with Him (compare Luke 19:11-26; Revelation 2:26; 3:21). While all Christians will be in His kingdom, only those who endure in this life will be a part of His kingdom administration. Since serving Christ is what we will do in eternity (Revelation 22:3), increased opportunity to serve Him should be extremely desirable. What a privilege to serve the King of kings by being a ruler over a city, county, state, or even country.[2]

While eternal life is free, eternal rulership will cost us persistent hard work, but "if we endure, we shall also reign with Him."

— Christians Who Deny Christ —

"If we deny Him, He also will deny us." Some think that Paul is threatening believers who deny Christ with eternal damnation. That, however, is completely contrary to the first half of verse 12 and to the context of verses 11 and 13.

The second half of verse 12 is antithetically parallel to the first half. After the words "If we endure, we shall also reign with Him," we expect, "If we don't endure, we shall not reign with Him." Yet that is precisely what verse 12b *is* saying. To deny Christ is to fail to endure in the faith. To be denied by Him is to be refused the privilege of ruling with Him.

Why didn't Paul just keep it simple by saying, "If we fail to endure, we won't reign"? It would seem that he is using the second half of verse 12 to paraphrase the Lord Jesus' words recorded in Matthew 10:33, "But whoever denies Me before men, him I will also deny before My Father who is in heaven."

At the Judgment Seat, the Lord Jesus will confess those believers who have openly confessed Him before others. "Therefore whoever confesses Me before men, him I will also confess before My Father who is in heaven" (Matthew 10:32). Thus Paul's implicit exhortation to endure in the first half of verse 12 includes the idea of confessing Christ before others. Probably the reason Paul spoke of enduring rather than confessing is because endurance suggests obedience on many fronts, including acknowledging Christ.

All who endure in their Christian lives will rule with Christ. However, as the second half of the verse brings out, endurance in confessing Christ is the *minimum* requirement. If one merely endures in his profession of Christ, he will rule.[3] However, Paul is calling for more than minimal endurance and reward. He wants Timothy, and all of us, to excel in the Christian life now and in rulership in the life to come.

Sadly, not all Christians openly confess Christ. Surely all of us have failed at this from time to time, but what Paul has in mind is a believer who has ceased to name the name of Christ publicly. If before we die or are raptured, we have become silent about our faith, we will not be confessed by Christ and we will not rule with Him.

How can a believer deny Christ before others? One obvious way is to cease going to church. Church is a very public way in which believers confess the name of Christ (Hebrews 10:23-25).

We err if we think this passage primarily relates to passing out gospel tracts or doing door-to-door evangelism. While those are forms of confessing Christ, neither was done at the time of Christ and Paul. Rather, what is obvious is that when the name of Jesus is mentioned, we must not shrink back as Peter did when he claimed he didn't know Jesus on the night of His betrayal. We must not live like Nicodemus, a member of the Sanhedrin who was a secret disciple of Christ (John 19:38-39). We should be open followers of Christ.

Who will be fit to reign with Christ? Only believers who endure in their confession of Him.

— Be a Nike Christian —

Coach Bill Bowerman was a legend at the University of Oregon. Steve Prefontaine, one of America's greatest distance runners, rose to prominence under Bowerman's direction.

In 1964 Bowerman teamed with one of his former students, Phil Knight, to form a company called Blue Ribbon Sports.

Eight years later, with Knight at the helm as President and CEO, Blue Ribbon Sports became Nike, Inc. named after the Greek goddess of victory.[4]

The expression "He who overcomes" (Revelation 2:26; 3:21), actually translates the Greek verb, *nikaō,*[5] the noun form of the word *nikē*. The verb and noun refer to winning, being victorious, and overcoming an opponent.

Before he died in a tragic automobile accident at the age of twenty-four, Steve Prefontaine used to speak to crowds of young athletes. "To give anything less than your best is to sacrifice the gift" became one of his famous appeals. On Nike's website you will find these words, "It was his spirit that helped set our course."[6]

The Nike swoosh has come to symbolize victory. For Nike, doing one's best *is* victory. The same should be true of every Christian; we are winners if we do our best for Jesus Christ.[7]

A Nike Christian is an overcomer, one who perseveres in faith and good works. That is what we are called to be. The Holy Spirit enables all believers to be victorious (2 Peter 1:3), but victory is not automatic. We must be doers of the Word, and not hearers only, if we are to be Nike Christians (James 1:22).

The apostle Paul often related the Christian life to athletic competition. As he faced execution for his faith he wrote, "I have fought the good fight, I have finished the race, I have kept the faith" (2 Timothy 4:7). That was Paul's aim (see 1 Corinthians 9:24-27), and it should be the aim of every Christian.

Whenever you see the Nike name, I hope you will call to mind its meaning—*overcomer*. And let that remind you that Jesus is coming soon and His reward is with Him (Revelation 22:12). Never forget that victorious Christians will rule with Christ. So be a Nike Christian!

---

[1] Since God credits us with dying with Christ, He also changes our nature. Believers are no longer slaves of sin (Romans 6:7). Rather, born again people are slaves of righteousness (Romans 6:18). This means that we no longer need to live the way we once did. Of course, success is not guaranteed simply because we

have the ability to obey. The believers in Corinth were still living like the unsaved five years after their new birth (1 Corinthians 3:3). It should be noted that Paul is not bringing out this aspect of our co-crucifixion with Christ. For in this context he is stressing the security associated with our death with Christ.

² Rulership probably will also include management that we don't normally think of as political. See Chapter 10, especially the section "Rulers in the Life to Come," for a discussion of other types of ruling with Christ.

³ He will rule provided he doesn't disqualify himself by willful indulgence in sin as Galatians 5:19-21 shows.

⁴ The history of Nike, Inc. can be found at their website (nikebiz.com).

⁵ The actual expression in Greek is *ho nikōn*. It is a substantive participle that functions as a noun. This can be translated "the one who overcomes," or even, "the victor" or "the winner." Jesus wants every Christian to be a winner in life.

⁶ For more on the life of Steve Prefontaine, see http://www.nike.com/ nikebiz/nikebiz.jhtml?page=5&item=steve.

⁷ There are degrees of overcomers. All who endure are overcomers. But since it is possible to do less than our best, some overcomers will be more highly rewarded than others. Compare verses 17 and 19 in Luke 19 to see the different commendation and reward given to two overcomers, one who maximized his life, and one who did not.

— Chapter 7 —

CROSS BEARERS
Matthew 16:24-28

The 1993 movie *Indecent Proposal* didn't do too well at the box office. Many moviegoers, including me, missed it. However, it had an interesting premise. According to the movie plot summary:

> A young couple very much in love are married and have started their respective careers…When the recession hits, they stand to lose everything they own, so they go to Vegas to have one shot at winning the money they need. After losing at the tables, they are approached by a millionaire who offers them a million dollars for a night with the wife.

I understand that the couple agreed to this indecent proposal. Under the right circumstances and with the right amount of money, they caved in to immorality. In other words, they could be bought.

— Justification by Self-Denial? —

A few years ago I received an e-mail message inviting me to check out a dissertation on Jesus' method of evangelism. That dissertation included a section on the Lord's gospel message where the author discussed the passage we are considering. He wrote:

> The teachings of Christ in Matthew 16:24-28 (cf. Lk. 9:23-34) make it clear that self-denial, an essential of obedience, is necessary for finding salvation...
>
> So, then, faith and obedience are taught by the Lord not only as ways to eternal life, but as requirements. In order for a man to inherit eternal life he must: believe in Jesus and practice obedience to God.[1]

That is a remarkable claim. Is faith in Christ the only condition of eternal salvation? Or, are self-denial and obedience to God's commands also required, as this writer suggests? Let's look at the entire passage:

> *Then Jesus said to His disciples, "If anyone desires to come after Me, let him deny himself, and take up his cross, and follow Me. For whoever desires to save his life will lose it, and whoever loses his life for My sake will find it. For what is a man profited if he gains the whole world, and loses his own soul? Or what will a man give in exchange for his soul? For the Son of Man will come in the glory of*

His Father with His angels, and then He will re-
ward each according to his works. Assuredly, I say
to you, there are some standing here who shall not
taste death till they see the Son of Man coming in
His kingdom. "

—Matthew 16:24-28

While I don't agree with the interpretations of Matthew 16:24-28 in that dissertation, I can understand why someone might draw those conclusions. Admittedly, this passage does seem to present a different gospel than John 3:16, which conditions eternal life solely on believing in Christ. Here we find the need to deny oneself, take up one's cross, and follow Christ. This passage also seems to contradict verses like Ephesians 2:8-9, which says that salvation is "not of works, lest anyone should boast." Yet Matthew 16:27 says, "He will reward each *according to his works*" (emphasis mine).

What gives here? We know that Scripture cannot contradict itself. The Bible is God's Word and is completely consistent.

— The Meaning of *Psychē* —

A proper understanding of the usage of the Greek word *psychē*, is crucial in order to correctly interpret this passage.

Psychē appears four times in these verses. Twice it is translated as "life" and twice as "soul." This unfortunate translation decision causes the English reader to think that a different Greek word is being used and a different meaning intended.

Here are those four uses with the Greek word *psychē* inserted instead of its translation:

(1) Whoever desires to save his *psychē* will lose it.

(2) Whoever loses his *psychē* for Christ's sake will find it.

(3) What is a man profited if he gains the whole world and loses his own *psychē?*

(4) What will a man give in exchange for his *psychē?*

What did the Lord mean here by the expression *saving* (or *losing*) *one's psychē?*

Some, like the writer of the dissertation, understand the expression *saving one's psychē* here and in the parallel texts in Matthew 10:38, Mark 8:34, and Luke 9:23 and 14:27, to refer to obtaining eternal salvation from hell. One author writes, "There is no salvation apart from cross-bearing."[2] Another writes, "Thus in a sense we pay the ultimate price for salvation when our sinful self is nailed to a cross. It is total abandonment of self-will....It denotes implicit obedience, full surrender to the lordship of Christ."[3]

— Salvation Is Not for Sale —

Others, including myself, understand this expression quite differently here and in the parallel texts. There are three major reasons why the eternal salvation view is untenable.

Self-denial and Cross-bearing Are Not Gospel Terms

Nowhere in Scripture is eternal salvation conditioned upon self-denial and cross-bearing. Justification is unmerited. It is by grace through faith, not of works (Ephesians 2:9; Romans 4:1-5; Titus 3:5).

Believers Already Have Eternal Life

The disciples (and especially Peter), are being addressed here. They were already believers (Matthew 16:16-17; see also John 2:11).[4] Since eternal salvation can't be lost (John 6:35-40; 10:27-30), the Lord must be warning the disciples about the possibility of losing something else.

Some might wonder how the disciples could have eternal life prior to the cross. After all, eternal redemption had not yet been purchased. However, 2,000 years before the cross, "Abraham believed God, and it was accounted to him for righteousness" (Genesis 15:6; Romans 4:3). God applied the work of the cross to anyone who believed in the Messiah for everlasting life—even before Jesus died. No strings attached.

Eternal Life Is Not a Recompense for Deeds Done

Recompense according to one's deeds (Matthew 16:27) is *not* a justification concept. Rather, it is a rewards concept. Jesus said, "For the Son of Man will come in the glory of His Father with His angels, *and then He will reward each according to his works*" (emphasis mine). Compare especially 2 Corinthians 5:10, a passage that clearly deals with a future works judgment of people who are already eternally secure. It reads:

> *For we must all appear before the judgment seat of Christ,* that each one may receive the things done in the body, *according to what he has done, whether good or bad* (emphasis mine).

Eternal life is absolutely free. Eternal rewards are not.

This leads us to the crucial question: What, then, is the Lord Jesus talking about when He speaks of saving one's *psychē?*

— Developing Our Eternal Capacity —

The expression *saving the psychē* in both the Septuagint and the Greek New Testament often refers to preserving one's physical life[5] or to gaining eternal rewards.[6]

All believers have eternal life. However, only self-denying believers will realize *the full potential of eternal life* both in this life and in the life to come (John 10:10; 1 Timothy 4:8).

Suffering precedes glory in God's plan. It did for our Lord and it will for His followers as well. If any believer wants to share fully in Christ's glory when He returns with His angels (verse 27), then suffering for Him now is imperative. We must give to receive. We must lose to gain.

Jesus told the disciples that some of them would not taste death until they saw Him coming in His kingdom (verse 28). We learn in the verses that follow (Matthew 17:1-8) that the three disciples who were closest to Jesus—Peter, James, and John—*did* see Him coming in His kingdom a week later when He was transformed in their presence on the Mount of Transfiguration.

They saw Him in a way they never had before because His glory had been hidden from them. Now they caught a glimpse of what He looked like, "His face shone like the sun, and His clothes became as white as the light" (Matthew 17:2).

The degree to which Jesus will share His glory with believers is related to how much we give of ourselves now. Peter later wrote,

> *But rejoice to the extent that you partake of Christ's*
> *sufferings, that* when His glory is revealed, *you*
> *may also be glad with exceeding joy.*
> —1 Peter 4:13 (emphasis mine)

Peter had seen a foretaste of that glory and he knew what was at stake. Any time a believer suffers in order to obey and serve God, he is losing his life that he may gain it.

Dr. Earl Radmacher illustrates this concept with cups. Some hold a lot. Others, like demitasse cups, hold very little. In this life we are developing our capacity to serve God. Believers who give up their lives for Christ develop a large capacity to serve and to live.

— Application —

How can a believer lose his life (i.e., deny himself and take up his cross) for the sake of Christ? By sharing in our Lord's sufferings.

One of the most common ways that committed believers suffer is through the pain we feel from living in this sinful world. Lot was called *righteous* by Peter because the wickedness around him "tormented his righteous soul day to day by seeing and hearing their lawless deeds" (2 Peter 2:8). Similarly Paul said, "For I consider that the sufferings of this present time are not worthy to be compared with the glory which shall be revealed in us" (Romans 8:18). Also, "...we ourselves groan within ourselves, eagerly waiting for the adoption, the redemption of our body" (Romans 8:23).

The *world* says that you can never have enough. The *Word* says that in order to gain a full experience of life you must give up living primarily for the present. In doing so, you may experience suffering. People at work may ridicule you because you share your faith, because your language is different, and you don't laugh at some of their jokes.

Your house and possessions may not be as grand as they could be because you give sacrificially to the Lord's work. You may pay more in taxes than others who make the same salary and deductions, because you don't cheat. You may give up much if you leave parents and hometown to serve the Lord in other parts of the country or abroad. You may even be martyred for your testimony.

If you could possess the wealth of the entire world for the rest of your life on the condition that you sacrifice the quality of your experience in God's kingdom forever, would you do it? Can you be bought?

In order to have a full experience of life now and forever, we must willingly give up our lives in service to God. The world may call us fools. But as martyred missionary Jim Elliot wrote in a now famous journal entry, "He is no fool who gives what he cannot keep to gain that which he cannot lose."[7]

---

[1] Paul S. Dixon, *The Evangelism of Christ: A Model for Evangelism Today*, Section 3 ("The Beliefs of Christ Regarding Evangelism"), under "The Requirements of Both Faith and Obedience." See http://members.aol.com/dixonps/ Evangelism_of_Christ.html.

[2] James Montgomery Boice, *Christ's Call to Discipleship* (Chicago: Moody Press, 1986), 36.

[3] John F. MacArthur, Jr., *The Gospel According to Jesus: What Does Jesus Mean When He Says, "Follow Me"?* (Grand Rapids: Zondervan Publishing House, 1988), 140. N.B. In the revised and expanded edition (Grand Rapids: Zondervan Publishing House, 1994), 147, the wording is slightly different, but the message is the same.

[4] Judas, of course, never came to faith in Christ and was an example of an unbelieving disciple. Among the twelve, he was the only one who wasn't a believer (see John 13:10).

[5] Compare Psalm 22:20-21; Proverbs 16:17; Ezekiel 18:27; Matthew 2:20; 20:28; Acts 27:37; 1 Peter 3:20; James 5:19-20.

[6] Compare Colossians 3:23-24; 1 Peter 1:9; Revelation 12:11; 20:4. All of the verses cited here and in n. 5 contain the Greek word *psychē*. However, in the English translations the word *soul* is often not present. Many times the word *life* is given instead. This, of course, supports the point being made here that saving the *psychē* doesn't refer to eternal salvation from hell. In addition, it should be noted that in some of these passages the words *save* or *lose* are not present. However, in each case the *concept* of saving or losing the life is present.

[7] The journal entry was from October 28, 1949, six years and a little more than a month before he was martyred by the Auca Indians in Ecuador on January 8, 1956 at the age of 28. A photocopy of the actual journal entry can be found at http://www.wheaton.edu/bgc/archives/faq/20.htm. For more information on Jim Elliot, see also http://www.christianmissions.net/bios/jelliot.html, and http://www.intouch.org/myintouch/mighty/portraits/jim_elliot_213678.html.

— Chapter 8 —

HUMBLE FOLLOWERS
Luke 17:7-10

On August 14, 2001 the Dallas Cowboys released starting quarterback Tony Banks. Among other things, he was asked by reporters if he hadn't turned down more money elsewhere to play with the Cowboys in the first place. He indicated that he chose Dallas not for the money, but for the chance to start and prove himself. He said, "That's the only reason I was playing for pennies, because I thought I was going to get a fair shake."

At the time, Banks's salary was $500,000 per year. While that isn't much for an NFL starting quarterback, most people would love to earn that many "pennies" every year. A few years at that level would set someone for life.

In the old days of professional sports, players had jobs in the off-season to supplement their salaries. They were truly playing for the love of the game.

Today, many professional athletes seem to view their exorbitant salaries as their due and not as a wonderful blessing. This is unfortunate. It has resulted in many becoming arrogant, aloof and, in many cases, less than fully committed to doing their best.

Christians must beware of this same trap. We may wonder why we are suffering so much as believers. Why don't we have more money, better houses, finer clothes, newer cars, etc.?

Servants of Christ should avoid developing an entitlement mentality. We are to be humble and self-effacing. Jesus spoke of the need of His servants to have such an attitude in Luke 17:7-10. Some understand this passage to mean that there will be no eternal rewards. However, the Lord is not denying here that He will reward faithfulness on the part of His servants. Instead, He is talking about what sort of attitude we, as His servants, should have.

— We Are His Servants —

After teaching the disciples about the need to forgive others (Luke 17:1-4) and to believe Him more (Luke 17:5-6), that is, to believe more of what He says in His Word, the Lord taught them about the proper attitude His servants should have (verses 7-10).

When a servant came in from the field late in the afternoon, his master said, "Prepare something for my supper, and gird yourself and serve me till I have eaten and drunk, and afterward you will eat and drink" (Luke 17:8).

The Lord then asked, "Does he thank that servant because he did the things that were commanded him? I think not" (verse 9). The word translated "thank" could also be translated as "favor" or even "reward." It is the famous word *charis* that is often translated as "grace." The question means something like this, "Did he *show favor toward* [*reward*] that servant because he did the things that were commanded?"

What's going on here? Does the Lord mean that masters should not thank or reward their servants? Or, to put it in a modern context, that employers shouldn't thank and reward their employees when they do a good job? Of course not.

We have the Lord's teaching backwards if we see the lesson directed to what the masters/employers should do or what their attitude should be. Rather, He was focusing on what the attitude of His servants should be. All believers are servants of Christ. What attitude then should a servant of Christ have concerning rewards?

— A Servant Should Serve Humbly —

The proper attitude we should have is given in the last verse.

> *So likewise you, when you have done all things which you are commanded, say, "We are unprofitable servants. We have done what was our duty to do."*

> —Luke 17:10

God *does not need to obligate Himself to reward us.* We are His servants and He could simply require us to serve, and discipline us when we don't.

Yet God *does obligate Himself.* He chooses to give rewards. This is demonstrated in many other passages. In Luke 19:17, the Lord says, "Well done, good servant; because you were faithful in a very little, have authority over ten cities." That is both praise and reward. Or, in Revelation 22:12, "And behold, I am coming quickly, and My reward is with Me, to give to every one according to his work." There is no doubt that the Lord Jesus will reward His servants.

May we never forget that the best thing anyone can say about us is that we are servants of the Lord Jesus Christ. That will be our eternal vocation (Revelation 22:3). Whether or not we receive rewards, our status does not change. Now and forever we will serve the King of kings and Lord of lords. That is an exciting future, because being His servant is better than anything else we could possibly do.

— Conclusion —

Mrs. Lamb was probably the best first grade teacher anyone has ever had. As her student, I was responsible to complete the assignments that she gave me. She didn't have to reward good work with anything other than grades, but she did. She heaped praise on all of us in her class when we did well. There was always a candy bar waiting each time we finished reading another book.

And the neatest thing is that she would put us on her lap in front of the whole class and just make a big fuss over the fact that we'd read another book.

That wonderful teacher made me want to come to school. I longed to receive her praise. How much more wonderful it will be to hear the praise of the Lamb of God who took away my sins by shedding His blood on Calvary.

While the Lord will reward believers, He is obligated to do so only because He *chooses* to obligate Himself. That He does so should motivate us to honor Him that much more.

Haughtiness is one of the things God hates most (Proverbs 6:16-17). Humility before God is crucial for the one who wishes to be rewarded. What a blessing it is that God chooses to reward His humble servants.

We should all serve Him regardless of any reward we might obtain. He has done so much for us that we should be overflowing with gratitude and delight in serving such a wonderful Master.

Isn't it great to know that the Lord is not only our Master, but our Friend as well, if we obey Him (John 15:14)? And isn't it encouraging to know there will be praise and reward for those who have served Him well?

I'd serve Him without any eternal rewards. I trust you would as well. But knowing that there will be rewards should heighten our love for Him and our motivation to do our duty.

~ Section 3 ~

WHAT ARE THE REWARDS?

If we endure,
We shall also reign with Him.
2 Timothy 2:12a

— Chapter 9 —

HEAVENLY TREASURE

S tar athlete, heir to a large fortune, and top graduate of one of the greatest universities in the world, Charles Thomas Studd had it all. To top it off, he was good looking and full of charisma. Yet none of those things was his greatest asset. You see, as a believer in Jesus Christ, C. T. was more focused on the life to come than this one. That is rare for any person. It is especially rare for a young man with his wealth and stature.

When he graduated from Cambridge University, he gave up his sport, fame, fortune, and even his homeland, to become a missionary in China, India, and finally inland Africa. C. T. served Christ on the mission field from 1885 until his death in 1931.

Where is your treasure? What is your aim in life? A recent study shows that there are over 50,000 people worldwide worth more than $30 million. Would your life be a success if you became one of those 50,000?

Early in our marriage my wife and I were invited to a Christian meeting. When we got there we met several other couples along with our friend and the speaker. The speaker asked what would make us really happy. One man raised his hand and said, "I'd really love to have a Porsche." So the speaker wrote "Porsche" on the board. A woman said, "I want to be a millionaire." So he wrote, "$1,000,000." Soon were added "Yacht," "Cruise around the world," and so forth.

Sharon and I sat there perplexed. While we wouldn't have minded any of those things, we knew that having them would not make us happy or fulfilled.

— The Problem with Treasure on Earth —

This problem of earthly treasure has plagued man throughout history. The pyramids contain the bodies of pharaohs who were buried with gold, diamonds, chariots, fine clothes, and even servants (who were buried alive!). Their idea was to take their treasure with them to the next life.

However, earthly possessions are extremely perishable. The Lord Jesus put it this way,

> *Do not lay up for yourselves treasures on earth, where moth and rust destroy and where thieves break in and steal.*
> —Matthew 6:19

Though the Lord gives just three examples of the fleeting nature of treasures in this life, many more could be added. We've all had moths eat holes in our clothes. (I generally get about two years out of a running shirt before holes mysteriously appear.)

Rust has eaten away at our possessions made of metal. (Recently the chassis of my lawn mower nearly disintegrated from rust.) Thieves have stolen from us. (My wife's purse and wedding ring were taken when we'd been married five years.)

The fence in our yard is decaying badly. If we don't fix it soon, it will likely fall down. The fact is our earthly "treasures" steadily decay without constant repair.

— The Beauty of Treasure in Heaven —

Whereas earthly treasure decays, heavenly treasure is imperishable. The Lord went on to say,

> *But lay up for yourselves treasures in heaven, where neither moth nor rust destroys and where thieves do not break in and steal.*
>
> —Matthew 6:20

Treasure laid up in heaven is not subject to decay. Moths, rust, and thieves can't touch it. Neither can anything else. It is permanent.

Treasure we lay up in heaven is currently being reserved for us, to be given to us at the Judgment Seat of Christ for our use in the kingdom of God. While many think of this treasure as a figure of speech for some unspecified blessings, I see it as an eternal trust fund that believers will use to glorify God. The more we have stored up, the more we can give away in service to the Lord.

What? Who would need money in the kingdom? Well, no one, if the kingdom of God were going to be some ethereal experience, consisting of floating on clouds and strumming harps. However, the description of the eternal kingdom on the new earth in Revelation 21:24 strongly suggests the existence of an economy. "The kings of the earth [will] bring their glory and honor into it [the New Jerusalem]." Actually the majority of manuscripts read, "The kings of the earth [will] bring the glory and honor of the nations to Him."

In any case, the point is clear. The three wise men who brought gifts to the baby Jesus were types of rulers who, in the age to come, will forever bring gold and other treasures to the Lord Jesus.

— Your Heart Is Where Your Treasure Is —

The reason many believers aren't concerned with laying up treasure in heaven is because they're too preoccupied with laying it up here. They aren't aware that something much better exists. The Lord Jesus said,

> *For where your treasure is, there your heart will be also.*
> —Matthew 6:21

It is impossible to make it your aim to lay up treasure on this earth, and at the same time have your heart set on the things of

God and the life to come.[1] What you value most is where your affections will be directed.

A few years ago, world-class athletes were asked the following question: "If you could take a drug that would cause you to win a gold medal, but it would kill you in ten years, would you take it?" Amazingly, the majority said yes. They'd sacrifice fifty or more years of life for a gold medal.

What would you give up to have treasure in heaven? Would you drive a lesser car than you could otherwise afford? Live in a more modest home? Have a less expensive wardrobe? Enjoy simpler or fewer vacations? Give up fifty years of life (if called upon to be a martyr, for example)? The answer you give to these questions will depend on where your heart is.

— Heavenly Treasure and Eternal Rewards —

I talk a lot in this book about eternal rewards. Treasure reserved in heaven is just one of the many *types* of rewards that God will give. However, it differs from the other rewards in one major way: *it is guaranteed the moment it is laid up.* Every time you do a good deed with a proper motive, a deposit is made to your account in the Bank of Heaven (Matthew 10:42). The more deposits you make, the more treasure you'll have with which to glorify God.

All other rewards will be given only to those who persevere in their service for Christ to the end of their lives. Those rewards include ruling with Christ, wearing white garments, the right to eat the hidden manna and the fruit of the tree of life, the right to enter the New Jerusalem by its gates, and a special name engraved on a beautiful white stone (Revelation 2:17; 3:4-5, 21; 22:14).[2]

There will be degrees of some or possibly all of these perseverance rewards. Some will rule, for example, over more cities than others. But all who persevere will rule. The garments of some may shine more brightly than others (Matthew 17:2). But all who persevere will wear radiant garments.

— Conclusion —

At the age of twenty-five, C. T. Studd received a large inheritance. He chose to give away nearly the entire estate—an amount approaching $2,000,000 in today's dollars. Later, he and his wife Priscilla gave away the remainder of his inheritance.[3] C. T. and Priscilla believed what the Lord Jesus said. They were more concerned with laying up eternal treasure in heaven than having earthly treasure now.

Few of us have the fame and fortune of C. T. Studd. Still, all of us are tempted to live for the treasures this world has to offer. C. T. is famous for having said, "If Jesus Christ is God and died for me, then no sacrifice can be too great for me to make for Him." That is powerful stuff.

A proper view of treasure is an antidote to spiritual lethargy. Earthly treasure is guaranteed to perish. Treasure reserved for us in heaven will last forever. Focusing our affections on the riches of the life to come is a powerful way to energize our Christian lives. "For where your treasure is, there your heart will be also."

---

[1] Just three verses later, the Lord Jesus made this point explicitly, saying: "No one can serve two masters; for either he will hate the one and love the other, or else he will be loyal to the one and despise the other. You cannot serve God and mammon [riches]" (Matthew 6:24).

[2] For a discussion of Revelation 3:5, see my book *Confident in Christ* (Irving, TX: Grace Evangelical Society, 1999), 119-27.

[3] See www.wholesomewords.org/missions/biostudd.html, p. 3.

— Chapter 10 —

RULING WITH CHRIST

According to the Department of Labor, the United States has 5,051,000 local government employees, 2,410,000 state government employees, and 4,477,000 federal government employees.[1]

Additionally, according to BizStats.com, there are over 24 million businesses in the U.S., the majority of which are sole proprietorships (17.5 million). Add to that number 1.3 million partnerships and 4.8 million corporations. That adds up to a lot more people in various levels of leadership.

One day the Lord Jesus is going to rule the entire world from the capital in Jerusalem. Many of His subjects will rule with Him. In the life to come, not all believers will have this opportunity. Only those who have earned that right will be in positions of authority.

— A Lack of Ambition to Rule —

I've met Christians who've told me that ruling with Christ just doesn't interest them. When pressed for a reason, their answers are usually vague. For the most part, they don't want to be in a position of authority over other people. Either they aren't supervisors at work (and don't want to be in the kingdom), or they *are* supervisors at work and don't like all the hassles involved in leading others.

Having a position of authority in this life is one thing. Ruling with Christ in the life to come is another.

Positions of authority in this life do give us a greater platform to glorify God. Consider, for example, the influence that stay-at-home moms have over their children. Training children to become godly adults is a huge responsibility that certainly glorifies God. However, any supervisory role in this life, even over one's children, is less than ideal, because both the supervisor and the ones being supervised are sinners. In the eternal kingdom there will be no sinners. Thus ruling with Christ will be far more satisfying and enjoyable, than supervising people in this life.

— Co-Heirs with Christ —

The idea of inheriting the kingdom and being a co-heir with Christ is one way the Bible speaks of ruling with Christ. We find this in a number of passages, as we shall now see.

All believers are children of God and hence heirs of God. "The Spirit Himself bears witness with our spirit that we are children of God, and if children, then heirs—heirs of God" (Romans 8:16-17a). However, not all believers will be co-heirs with Christ in the life to come. Only those who suffer with Him will earn the right to inherit the kingdom with Him. The passage just cited continues as follows: "…and joint heirs with Christ, if indeed we suffer with Him, that we may also be glorified together" (Romans 8:17b).

Believers are called to work heartily for the Lord that they may win the inheritance of ruling with Christ.

> *And whatever you do, do it heartily, as to the Lord and not to men, knowing that from the Lord you will receive the reward of the inheritance; for you serve the Lord Christ. But he who does wrong will be repaid for the wrong which he has done, and there is no partiality.*
> —Colossians 3:23-25

Paul presents two options for the believer. The believer who heartily serves God will receive the reward which is the inheritance of ruling with Christ. The believer who is unrighteous[2] in his behavior will not gain the inheritance, but will reap shame and rebuke instead.

Many other passages deal with the inheritance of ruling with Christ, or what I call *active inheritance*. The following are some to consider: Matthew 5:5; 19:29; 25:34; 1 Corinthians 6:9-11;

15:50; Galatians 5:19-21; Ephesians 5:5-7; Hebrews 1:14; 6:12; James 2:5; 1 Peter 1:4.[3]

I have a relative who was disinherited by her parents. She was still a member of the family and attended all of their gatherings. She was still much loved. But she was written out of the will. When the time came to inherit the assets of the parents, she received none.

So it is with some believers. All believers are members of the family of God. But only some will gain the inheritance of being co-heirs with Christ and ruling with Him in the life to come.

— To Be His Partner —

The Greek word *metochos* means *partner* or *partaker*. The term is used in a secular sense once in the New Testament to refer to Peter, James, and John, who, prior to following Jesus, had been *partners* in their fishing business (Luke 5:7).

All other New Testament uses of this term occur in Hebrews. Two of the five uses in Hebrews refer to being a "partaker" or "recipient" of the Holy Spirit (6:4) and of discipline (12:8). The remaining three refer to the potential future role of believers with Christ (1:9; 3:1, 14). We may be His *partners* in the life to come. Imagine what a glorious life that would be! But that potential will become a reality only if we hold fast our confession of hope until He returns (Hebrews 10:23-25).

Have you ever thought about being one of Jesus' *partners* in the life to come? As in any endeavor, partners work together.

Thus partners of the King of kings are people who will share in His kingdom rule. They will not only be subjects in the kingdom, but they will also have special tasks to perform. They will have more authority and opportunity than others.

Believers who are partners of Christ will glorify Him more than those who are not. And as a result, their eternal experience will be more joyful (Hebrews 1:9).

— To Sit on His Throne —

Revelation 2–3 contains letters to seven churches. The penultimate verse in the seventh letter also serves to apply the message of all seven letters.

To him who overcomes I will grant to sit with Me on My throne, as I also overcame and sat down with My Father on His throne.
—Revelation 3:21

Sitting with the Lord on His throne is a figure for sharing in His kingdom rule.

—The Reign of Servant Leaders —

The Lord taught His disciples that those who rule in His kingdom will not lord it over their charges. Instead, they will be servant leaders.

> *The kings of the Gentiles exercise lordship over them, and those who exercise authority over them are called "benefactors." But not so among you; on the contrary, he who is greatest among you, let him be as the younger, and he who governs as he who serves...I am among you as the One who serves.*
> —Luke 22:25-27

The Lord illustrated this beautifully when He washed the feet of the disciples. After doing so He said, "For I have given you an example, that you should do as I have done to you...If you know these things, happy are you if you do them" (John 13:15, 17).

Jody Dillow's book *The Reign of the Servant Kings* captures this truth nicely. In Jesus' kingdom all rulers will be servant leaders. Rulership will not be arrogant domination, but humble direction, assistance, and service to others. Those who rule will delight in serving the Lord by serving His people and His program.

— Rulers in the Life to Come —

When I first became a Christian I had never heard of eternal rewards, and my concept of the kingdom was that we'd float on clouds and sing praise songs forever. Gradually I learned that our eternal destiny is not heaven, but the eternal kingdom that will be on the new earth (Revelation 21:1-3). Then I learned that we will do much more than sing, as glorious as that will be. We will serve Him forever (Revelation 22:3).

There is not room here to discuss in detail what the eternal kingdom will be like. I have, however, placed that discussion in Appendix 3, "What Will Eternity Be Like?," in case you want to learn more.

To imagine what eternity will be like, we should start in the Garden of Eden. If Adam and Eve had not sinned, they would have fulfilled their mandate to be fruitful and multiply, fill the earth and subdue it, and have dominion over all of creation (Genesis 1:28). They would have built cities, roads, vehicles, farms, ranches, buildings, and so on. In other words, they would have developed a beautiful society that would have forever become more and more glorious.

God will still realize that vision, in spite of the Fall. First, He will establish a glorious kingdom on this earth during the Millennium. Then, after mankind's final rebellion, He will destroy this world and create the new heavens and the new earth (2 Peter 3:10-13; Revelation 21–22). That new creation will be flawless, with no taint of the Fall remaining.

On the new earth, we will realize the purpose for which we were created.

Rulership will be quite varied. Some will hold positions of authority in the new world government: Presidents, Governors, Mayors, City Council members, Judges, Legislators, and the like. Others will have authority within commerce. Surely the kingdom will have transportation companies, publishers, architectural firms, developers, utilities, entertainment and sports companies, and so on. All of these businesses will need people in various levels of management.

The more authority a person has, the more he or she will be able to glorify the Lord Jesus.

— Conclusion —

One of the great rewards available to believers is ruling with Christ; this is also called being co-heirs with Christ, or being His partners.

We are becoming now what we will be forever. We should live each day in light of the glorious prospect of ruling with Christ.

---

[1] See http://data.bls.gov/cgi-bin/surveymost?en.

[2] The Greek word translated "he who does wrong" is *adikōn*. It could be translated "the unrighteous." Not all believers live righteously. The same word is used in another inheritance passage, 1 Corinthians 6:9-11. There Paul says that the unrighteous—the *adikoi*—will not inherit the kingdom of God. The main difference between the two passages is one uses the singular (*adikōn*) and the other the plural (*adikoi*).

[3] For more discussion of these passages see Joseph C. Dillow, *The Reign of the Servant Kings: A Study of Eternal Security and the Final Significance of Man* (Hayesville, NC: Schoettle Publishing Company, 1992), Zane C. Hodges, *Absolutely Free! A Biblical Reply to Lordship Salvation* (Dallas and Grand Rapids: Redención Viva and Zondervan Publishing House, 1989), *The Gospel Under Siege,* second edition (Dallas: Redención Viva, 1981, 1992), and *The Epistle of James: Proven Character Through Testing* (Irving, TX: Grace Evangelical Society, 1994), Charles Stanley, *Eternal Security* (Nashville: Thomas Nelson Publishers, 1990), and my book, *Confident in Christ* (Irving, TX: Grace Evangelical Society, 1999).

— Chapter 11 —

SPECIAL PRIVILEGES

Special privileges motivate people to do their best by lightening their burdens and giving them more energy to do the job at hand. To have an office as opposed to a cubicle is a nice upgrade. Add a window to the office and things have improved even more. Your own washroom, and maybe your own elevator, puts you in the executive category.

But is it only in this life that special privileges exist? Or is it possible that the eternal rewards God gives include special privileges as well?

— God-Honoring Clothing —

The Lord Jesus promises that overcoming believers "shall walk with Me in white, for they are worthy" (Revelation 3:4).[1] Because some believers in this life overcome the world, they are worthy of honor. One of those honors is to wear special white garments.

Keep in mind that the Lord Jesus Himself will be clothed in dazzling white garments that will outshine all others. His glory will be supreme.

When at the Mount of Transfiguration He appeared in His glory, "His clothes became as white as the light" (Matthew 17:2). Special clothing is not insignificant, because it honors a person. The more glorious the garments, the more honor to the wearer.

Like the sun, the Lord's garments will have maximum radiance. The garments of great servants like Moses, Elijah, Daniel, Deborah, Esther, and Mary will surely glow brightly. But theirs will be reflected glory, like the glory of the moon that reflects the glory of the sun.

Would you not want to be identified as closely as possible with the Lord Jesus and glorify Him, even in your clothing? The quality of your eternal garments will be determined by what you do in this life. Once this life is over, it will be too late to influence your worthiness to walk with Christ in white.

— Life-Enhancing Foods —

Food has multiple purposes in this life. Eating well increases one's energy and ability to function. In addition, food is one of life's pleasures. And, for the Christian in fellowship with God, the provision of food should increase our thankfulness to Him.

From the beginning God intended people to enjoy food. If Adam and Eve had not sinned, mankind would have forever eaten from the foods God provided. While many of us don't think of food in the life to come, we should.

At the Last Supper the Lord Jesus indicated He wouldn't drink of the fruit of the vine with His disciples again until He came in His kingdom. That means, of course, that He and they will enjoy drinking wine together in the kingdom.

After the Lord rose from the dead, He ate some fish and honey in the presence of His disciples (Luke 24:41-43). He also prepared fish for them and possibly shared that meal as well (John 21:9-15). Food will not be foreign to saints with glorified bodies. Surely all will eat, but some will enjoy special delicacies reserved only for persevering saints.

Two foods that will be reserved for believers who overcome in this life, are manna and the fruit of the tree of life.

The Lord said to the Church in Pergamos, "To him who overcomes I will give some of the hidden manna to eat" (Revelation 2:17). God fed Israel for forty years on manna (Exodus 16:15-16) and instructed them to put some away as a memorial to His provision. *Hidden manna* was that which was put away in the ark of the covenant (Hebrews 9:4). In eternity He will give manna to believers who overcame in this life.

This manna will surely provide the benefits good food offers today: increased energy, enhanced ability to serve God, and enjoyment. Eating that bread will forever remind us that the Lord Jesus is the Bread of Life (see John 6:35).

The Church at Ephesus heard this promise, "To him who overcomes I will give to eat from the tree of life, which is in the midst of the Paradise of God" (Revelation 2:7; see also 22:14). The tree of life was in the original Paradise, the Garden of Eden.

THE ROAD TO REWARD

It would have granted fullness of life to mankind if the Fall had not occurred. But if fallen men had eaten of it, they would have lived forever in unglorified bodies. So Adam and Eve were banished from the Garden. But the tree will flourish in the kingdom, providing a different fruit each month (Revelation 22:2), and enhancing the lives of those who eat of it. This special privilege is available only for believers who persevere.

— Special Entrance —

When my friend Al visited the Middle East, an Israeli tour guide told him about a VIP entrance into a Middle Eastern city which only special dignitaries were permitted to use. The New Jerusalem will have twelve such entrances.

It is quite probable that there will be more ways to enter the New Jerusalem than through its twelve gates of pearl. While all believers will be able to enter the city, only select believers will enter by the gates. "Blessed are those who do His commandments, that they may...enter through the gates into the city" (Revelation 22:14).

In the Old Testament to be "in the gates" was a privilege reserved for the elders of the city. Citizens would come there to ask the elders for their judgment in matters (see Ruth 4:9-10).

To enter the New Jerusalem through one of its twelve gates will be a great honor reserved only for those believers who overcame in this life.

— A New Name —

To have a good name is always important, and is especially so in the Bible. When God changed the names of people, their new names were significant. Jacob became Israel, Prince with God (Genesis 32:28). Simon became Peter, the Rock (Matthew 16:18).

A white stone engraved with a unique name will be given to every overcomer.

> *And I will give him a white stone, and on the stone a new name written which no one knows except him who receives it.*
> —Revelation 2:17

Imagine the joy of having a stone engraved with the Lord's special name for you!

One motivation to hang in there when things get tough now is to realize that our new name hangs in the balance.

— Fullness of Life —

The Lord Jesus said that He came that we might have life, and that we might have it more abundantly (John 10:10). All believers have eternal life now, but not all have the same abundance of that life. One who has walked with Christ for decades surely is experiencing a more abundant life than one who has walked with Him for a few days.

How much glory, honor, and authority we will have in the life to come is directly related to what we have done with our Christian lives. The more we do for Christ in this life, assuming our motives are right (see Matthew 6:1-21), the more abundant our eternal experience will be.

— These Privileges Benefit Everyone —

We must not think that these privileges are solely for the benefit of the recipient. We have been made to glorify God by loving and serving others. These privileges will enable overcomers to do just that. Thus everyone benefits and the Lord Himself will be pleased.

— Conclusion —

If the Lord wants you to have these privileges of a lifetime well spent, then it is a false spirituality that says, "Oh, I don't want any special privileges." You will, if you want for yourself what the Lord obviously desires for all His children.

---

[1] The next verse (Revelation 3:5) indicates that the Lord will not blot the name of the overcomer out of the Book of Life. That is an example of *litotes,* or understatement, because He won't blot anyone's name from the Book of Life. Rather, He is saying that He will pay tribute to the overcomer by giving him exalted garments and an exalted name.

— Chapter 12 —

HIS APPROVAL

My father died when I was thirty-seven. How I had longed for his approval, wanting him to be pleased with me and with what I had done with my life.

Sadly, that was not to be. My dad's father was an alcoholic and a perfectionist. My dad could never do enough to gain his father's approval. When he became a man and started his own family, he continued that legacy with my sisters and me.

Don't get me wrong. My dad loved me very much and made that clear, and yet he just couldn't approve of me. He accepted me, but his approval never came.

After my dad died in 1989, I found myself searching for others who would approve of me. Many men reminded me of my dad. But guess what—*they didn't approve of me either.*

One day I realized that the approval I was longing for is not from men, but from God. I want to hear the Lord Jesus say, "Well done, good servant" (Luke 19:17).

Many Christians fail to realize that it is possible to obtain God's approval. But, once they grasp this truth, it becomes a powerful force in their lives.

— Aiming for God's Approval —

Paul's aim in life was to gain the Lord's approval.

> *But I discipline my body and bring it into subjection, lest, when I have preached to others, I myself should become disqualified* [disapproved].
> —1 Corinthians 9:27

The Greek word translated "disqualified" is *adokimos*. The addition of the letter "a" before a word in Greek often negates it. We find the same thing in English. For example, the opposite of a *theist* is an *atheist*.

The word *dokimos* means "approved." For example, in 2 Timothy 2:15, the verse made famous by AWANA, Paul urged Timothy to be diligent to show himself an "approved" (*dokimos*) workman who need not be ashamed. Disapproved (*adokimos*) workmen will indeed be ashamed of themselves before Christ (compare 1 John 2:28).

You may wonder, what's the difference? If I'm sure I'm saved, then God approves of me, right? Wrong. Approval and acceptance are two different things in Scripture. Paul makes that clear in 1 Corinthians 9:24-27. He knew he had eternal life and was accepted by the Lord. But he was not sure he would persevere in the faith and maintain the Lord's approval.

God *accepts* all who have come to faith in Christ, no matter how they are living, or whether they are serving Him. Whether they pray, read the Word, or go to church. To have eternal life we must simply believe in Christ for it (John 6:47). However, to gain His *approval,* we must do more than believe in Christ (1 Corinthians 9:24-27).

If you are a good parent, you always *accept* your children. But does that mean you always *approve* of them? Of course not! What if one of your children were arrested for selling cocaine? You would still accept him, but you would *not* approve of him.

The Good Housekeeping Seal of Approval means that the Good Housekeeping Institute has evaluated a particular product and concluded that its quality is worthy of endorsement. So it is with God. If the Lord approves of you, He considers you a good servant; He commends you for what you are doing for Him.

— What Approval Will Mean —

Even if no additional privileges and rulership were available, His approval alone would be wonderful. Imagine going through eternity knowing that the Lord approved of you. You would forever delight in the memory of the day He told you, "Well done, good and faithful servant."

Of course, approval will grant one a special status in the kingdom. The approved will be a group of saints distinguished by their clothing, diet, and other privileges.

If you grew up in a functional home and received your dad's approval, you know this impacts every day of your life. It is part of who you are. If, like me, you grew up without it, that too is part of who you are. You can overcome it, of course, by developing your identity in Christ.

If you are walking in fellowship with Him, then currently you are approved by Him. If you maintain fellowship with Him, you will forever be one of the approved.

I can't stress enough how important it is that you live each day in light of eternity. He has given us all we need to gain His approval. The Holy Spirit lives within each believer and enables us to be godly persons (2 Peter 1:3), but it is *not* automatic. We must live by faith in Christ (Galatians 2:20), allowing God to transform our lives by the renewing of our minds (Romans 12:1-2; 2 Corinthians 3:18; Ephesians 4:23).

— Confidence or Shame? —

Those are our options when we appear before the Lord Jesus at His Judgment Seat. The apostle John put it this way:

> *And now, little children, abide in Him, that when He appears, we may have confidence and not be ashamed before Him at His coming.*
> —1 John 2:28

Certainly any shame the glorified saint experiences will be short-lived. However, what should be a glorious day of honor can in reality be a day of regret (compare 1 John 4:17-19; see also Chapter 5).

It is equally certain that the approved believer will forever have a special measure of confidence and joy.

Oh, how I want His approval.

— Chapter 13 —

FULLNESS FOREVER

When I was a child, I didn't have much patience for delayed gratification. A reward that was more than a day off motivated me little, if at all. As I matured I learned to delay gratification, and came to be highly motivated by rewards that were years away.

I planned on spending seven to eight years in seminary to get both my master's and doctoral degrees. That is a long time for a young man. Yet I hung in there because I was convinced that the degrees would have a positive impact on the rest of my life. Seven years of preparation was a small price to pay for an enhanced ability to understand, apply, and teach God's Word.

Businesses use various incentives to motivate people to do their best work. For people in sales, there are three types of prizes: cash, merchandise, and trips. Top managers are given cash bonuses as well as promotions, increased base salaries, and stock options.

Christianity offers incentives too. One of these is eternal reward. Although there are rewards now for the believer, most of them won't be given to us until after this life is over and we appear before the Judgment Seat of Christ. This may mean waiting decades to receive them.

Thus, the length of time these rewards will last once we receive them, makes a difference as to how motivated we will be to obtain them and how meaningful they will be to us once we do. Of those who believe in eternal rewards as an idea distinct from eternal salvation, there are three views concerning how long rewards last: a few minutes, a thousand years, or forever.

— A Few Minutes? —

Revelation 4:10-11 states,

> …the twenty-four elders fall down before Him who sits on the throne and worship Him who lives forever and ever, and cast their crowns before the throne, saying: "You are worthy, O Lord, To receive glory and honor and power; For You created all things, And by Your will they exist and were created."

Some Bible students are highly influenced by this passage, believing it to mean that all rewards given to believers by Christ will be returned to Him immediately after the Bema.[1]

In the first place, they argue that verse 10 says that, "the twenty-four elders…cast their crowns before the throne." Since crowns represent a type of eternal reward, the casting of crowns at Jesus' feet suggests to some that we will give our rewards back to Him immediately after receiving them.

In the second place, it is felt that verse 11 indicates that the casting down of crowns shows that all glory, honor, and power belong to the Lord Jesus. If we were to retain eternal rewards, we would be robbing the Lord of the glory, honor, and power that are uniquely His.

While on the surface these arguments might sound convincing, they really hold about as much water as a colander.

Concerning the casting down of crowns, most people forget that verse 10 is actually the middle of a sentence that begins at verse 9:

> Whenever *the living creatures give glory and honor and thanks to Him who sits on the throne, who lives forever and ever, the twenty-four elders fall down...and cast their crowns...* (emphasis mine).

Notice the word *whenever* in verse 9. The crown-casting in verse 10 is not a one-time event. It is repeated again and again. Indeed, *every* time the living creatures say, "Holy, holy, holy, Lord God Almighty, who was and is and is to come!" (verse 8b), then the twenty-four elders cast down their crowns. And according to the first half of verse 8, the living creatures "do not rest day or night..."

This crown-casting clearly does not refer to something believers are doing after the Judgment Seat of Christ. This is an ongoing event in which a small number of beings (angelic beings, in light of Revelation 7:11) participate.

While all glory, honor, and power come from the Lord Jesus, this in no way suggests He will not share these with others. Indeed, He promised to share these blessings with believers who persevere (compare Matthew 16:27; 2 Timothy 2:12; Hebrews 1:9; 1 Peter 4:13; Revelation 2:26; 3:21). Allowing humans to have some measure of glory, honor, and power in no way diminishes Christ's glory. If it did, Moses' face would never have shone. Elijah wouldn't have been taken up to heaven in a whirlwind and flaming chariot. David would never have been king of Israel. The Lord Jesus would not be called the Son of David. He would not have promised the apostles that they would rule over the twelve tribes of Israel. He wouldn't have given Adam and Eve and all of mankind dominion over the earth. And so on.

This view has nothing substantial to commend it. The only passage used to prove it fails to do so. Furthermore, other passages make it clear that rewards are lasting.

— One Thousand Years? —

Influenced by Revelation 20:4-6, others are convinced that rewards will last only as long as the Millennium.

> *And I saw thrones, and they sat on them, and judgment was committed to them. Then I saw the souls of those who had been beheaded for their witness to Jesus and for the word of God, who had*

not worshiped the beast or his image, and had not received his mark on their foreheads or on their hands. And they lived and reigned with Christ for a thousand years. But the rest of the dead did not live again until the thousand years were finished. This is the first resurrection. Blessed and holy is he who has part in the first resurrection. Over such the second death has no power, but they shall be priests of God and of Christ, and shall reign with Him a thousand years.

Twice in these verses we see that saints who were martyred during the Tribulation will rule with Christ for a thousand years. Many view this as concrete evidence that rewards will cease after the Millennium.

The problem with this view is that no verses can be cited, including Revelation 20:4-6, that *limit* rulership and the other rewards to the Millennium. While it is true that the rewards will be enjoyed *during* the Millennium, it is not necessarily true that they will end when it does.

— Forever? —

If even one passage made it clear that rewards are unending, the issue would be settled. The fact is we have not one, but many.

When Paul speaks of the prize, or crown, we are seeking, he says that it is *imperishable* (1 Corinthians 9:25), contrasting it with a *perishable* crown. If our rewards lasted for one thousand years, they would be *perishable*. Remember, with the Lord a thousand years is as but a single day. Yet Paul says this will be an *imperishable* crown. An *imperishable* crown is an eternal one![2]

The Lord Jesus commands us to lay up treasure in heaven (Matthew 6:19-21), where moths and rust can never destroy it, nor thieves steal it. Clearly these are descriptions intended to convey *permanence*.

Peter spoke of an imperishable and undefiled inheritance in 1 Peter 1:4. While most commentators take this verse to refer to eternal salvation, the context actually supports the view that the author had the matter of eternal rewards in mind.

In 1977 I spent a week with Josh McDowell while he spoke at Marshall University. At that time I thought 1 Peter 1:4 was a statement about eternal security. I'll never forget Josh's reply when I mentioned it. He said, "Yes, but those who reject eternal security will point out that Peter says that this inheritance is 'kept by the power of God *through faith*...' They will reply that ongoing faith is required."[3]

I've come to see that Josh's hypothetical objection is legitimate. Peter was not thinking of the initial faith by which one gains eternal life, nor was he making a point about eternal security. Rather, he was talking about the fact that the rewards that the Lord will give at the Bema will be eternal.

The readers, who were believers (1:2, 23; 2:7), were experiencing persecution (verse 6). Their faith would pass the test only if they persevered (verse 7). In that case they would gain "praise, honor, and glory at the revelation of Jesus Christ" (verse 7).[4]

In the Book of Revelation, it is clear that Christ's rewards will extend beyond the Millennium into the eternal kingdom. Revelation 21:24 speaks of the kings of the earth in the eternal kingdom. In Revelation 22:12 the Lord Jesus says:

> *And behold, I am coming quickly, and My reward is with Me, to give to every one according to his work.*

Overcoming Christians are then promised that they will be rewarded with "the right to the tree of life" (22:14a). They will also be permitted to enter the New Jerusalem by its twelve gates (22:14b). The tree of life and the New Jerusalem won't even *be* on earth until after the Millennium and the destruction of the current heavens and earth (compare Revelation 21:1-3).

— Ultimate Prizes —

Imagine if God guaranteed you $100 million here and now if you persevered in faith and good works for twenty years. I think the number desiring to serve the Lord would go up significantly.

Well, what if God offered something better than that? A person who received $100 million at age forty would have only a few decades to enjoy it. What if God offered rewards that last forever, not just for a few decades? Wouldn't that be far superior?

Ruling with Christ forever is priceless. The hidden manna and the fruits from the tree of life will be wonderful blessings. Treasure that is currently being stored up for us in heaven is something we will enjoy forever.

Many Christians place more hope on winning the lottery than they do on gaining meaningful eternal rewards. Either they are completely unaware of what God says, or they are convinced the rewards won't be that special.

Mary Decker Slaney is arguably the greatest female athlete the U.S. has ever produced, setting twenty-six U.S. and seventeen world records during her amazing career. In 1982 she was the top female runner in the world in all distances from 800 meters to 10,000 meters (one-half mile up to six miles). Due to an injury, she missed the 1976 Olympics. She missed the 1980 Olympics in Russia because of the U.S. boycott of the games. Favored to win the gold in both the 1,500 and 3,000 meters in the 1984 Los Angeles Olympics, Mary decided to compete only in the 3,000 meter race in order to reduce the risk of injury. In the finals of the 3,000 she was in the lead, running strong, and it appeared she would easily win the race. Then Zola Budd, a barefoot runner from South Africa, with little international experience, accidentally tripped Mary. Down to the track she went. As she was writhing in pain in the infield, the race went on without her.

Mary competed in the 1988 and 1996 Olympics, but failed to win any medals. During her career she underwent twenty leg, foot, and ankle operations in order to keep her running career alive. Imagine all the pain of the surgeries and recoveries. And anyone who has run track knows that the workouts are very painful, even for a healthy runner.

Mary had a drive within her that was intense. Her motivations were likely numerous: a love for running competitively, a desire for fame and fortune, the lure of the medals and the cheering crowds, and traveling around the world. For over twenty years she experienced these things.

The apostles were that intense in their service for Christ. And so should we all be. Our motivations are numerous as well: present blessings, avoiding God's discipline, gratitude, joy of service, a desire to please and glorify God, as well as a desire to gain eternal rewards.

Eternal rewards are eternal. They are the ultimate in delayed gratification. God guarantees it.

---

[1] One might legitimately wonder how a reward held for only a few minutes is truly a reward. Some of those holding this view respond by saying that while the rewards are ours for only a few minutes, we have eternal satisfaction and joy in knowing that we gave our crowns back to the Lord. Yet there is no text which says this. Additionally, as we shall see, there are many texts which directly indicate that we retain forever the rewards we receive.

[2] Of course, some might say that the crowns themselves are imperishable, yet we do not retain them. If we give them back to the Lord Jesus, He can keep them forever. However, the context of 1 Corinthians 9:24-27 does not support that possibility. Clearly Paul is thinking of a crown we retain forever. "Run in such a way that you may obtain it" (verse 24). If the crown were imperishable, but we would only keep it for a few minutes, his whole argument collapses. In that case the athlete who received the perishable crown actually enjoyed it longer than the believer who "obtained" an imperishable crown.

[3] The verse contained in this quote goes on to say, "for salvation ready to be revealed in the last time" (1 Peter 1:5). That salvation is spoken of again a few verses later, "receiving the end of your faith—the salvation of your souls" (verse 9). The saving of the soul is often used in Scripture to refer to physical deliverance from death. Compare 1 Peter 3:20 concerning the salvation of eight souls via Noah's ark. However, here it is clearly an eschatological salvation: "reserved in heaven...ready to be revealed in the last time." This salvation of the souls or lives of believers parallels Matthew 16:24-28 that also deals with eschatological salvation. (See Chapter 7.) Only those believers who persevere in faith and good works will rule with Christ in the life to come.

[4] See Joseph C. Dillow, *The Reign of the Servant Kings: A Study of Eternal Security and the Final Significance of Man* (Hayesville, NC: Schoettle Publishing Company, 1992), 572.

~ Section 4 ~

HOW SHOULD THIS IMPACT MY LIFE NOW?

Therefore I run thus:
not with uncertainty.
Thus I fight:
not as one who beats the air.
But I discipline my body
and bring it into subjection,
lest, when I have preached to others,
I myself should become disqualified.
1 Corinthians 9:26-27

— Chapter 14 —

PREPARE TO MEET THE JUDGE
James 5:9

Courtroom shows are fascinating. Why? They involve real-life drama that we can all relate to. As the evidence comes in, we form our own opinions of innocence or guilt and wonder how the judge will rule. A range of emotion washes over us: thankfulness for what we have, anger at unrepentant evil, a desire for justice, identification with the plaintiff or defendant, respect for the judge, as well as satisfaction in what we perceive is a fair verdict. No one viewing these shows would envy the role of a defendant clearly at fault. We wouldn't want our shortcomings to be revealed and judged!

I have appeared in court twice—for traffic violations. As a teenager I was ticketed for speeding and I went to court to try to avoid a fine. I stood before a judge, confessed my guilt, and apologized for breaking the law.

My second run-in with the law occurred in 1974, just days after the speed limit was reduced from 65 to 55. A graduate student at the time, I was driving to my teaching assistant job at a local junior college. The officer clocked me at 60, but my speedometer read 55. I thought I had kept to the speed limit. I had even seen the highway patrolman in my mirror. I decided to fight the ticket in court—and lost. The judge informed me that the patrol car speedometers are checked each month. "Yours is off," he said bluntly. "Get it fixed."

Like the police, we need to check our standards regularly. We may think that we are good judges of what is right and wrong, but if our standards disagree with those set forth in the Word of God, we are wrong. Like it or not, the Bible makes it clear that *every* person will have his or her day in court—unbelievers after the Millennium at the Great White Throne Judgment,[1] and believers before the Millennium at the Judgment Seat of Christ.[2]

— The Judge Is Coming —

We often speak of the Lord Jesus Christ as our *Savior*. But when is the last time you heard Him referred to as our *Judge*? Can't remember? Why is that? Maybe it's because it's sobering to think that we as believers are accountable for our actions. Whether we realize it or not, our Savior is returning someday as our Judge.

Many believers wrongly assume that because they have eternal life, they won't be judged for the things they have done as Christians. After all, if all their sin is covered under the blood of Christ, why does it matter how they live?[3] They might give lip service to living for Christ, but many Christians feel that if they are lax in their service, it won't really matter.

James, the half-brother of the Lord Jesus, was under no such illusion, having heard Jesus teach on this topic many times. He knew that all believers will be judged—but not to determine our eternal destiny, for Jesus promised we wouldn't come into judgment for that (John 5:24).[4] Yet there will be a time when all the words and deeds of Christians will be examined. James wrote:

> *Do not grumble against one another, brethren, lest you be condemned. Behold, the Judge is standing at the door!*
>
> —James 5:9

Grumbling against others is a problem for me. Even after thirty years as a believer, I still struggle with this, as do many Christians. Imagine standing before the Lord Jesus and having Him evaluate all you have said and done since you came to faith in Him for eternal life. There are a lot of things I've said and done that I'd just as soon the Judge not consider.

Isn't that the point James is making? We should live today in light of the fact that the Judge is at the door and ready to judge us for all we say and do. In his commentary on James, Zane Hodges states:

> This sense of the imminency of the Savior's return is captured in the striking metaphor, *Behold, the Judge is standing at the door.* Like a Roman lictor announcing a judge's impending entry, as it were, James cries, "Quiet!" His Christian readers must fully silence their complaints against one another in the realization that their

Lord and Judge can at any moment appear and sit down on the Bema (Judgment Seat) in order to assess their lives...They must therefore be careful that He does not find them nurturing a complaining spirit against their fellow believers. As Paul has so clearly stated, *So then each of us shall give account of himself to God. Therefore let us not judge one another anymore* (Rom 14:12-13a).[5]

There is great power in the following truths:

- Jesus could return for believers at any moment.

- When He comes, we will be judged. We can't hide from His judgment; He sees all.

- Our options are shame or confidence before our Lord (1 John 2:28).

- Only believers who are persevering in faith and good works will rule with Christ forever (e.g., 2 Timothy 2:12).

- The Lord Jesus is not only our Savior—He is also our Judge!

— The Motivation for Endurance —

In December 1998 I completed the Dallas White Rock Marathon in five hours and twenty-seven minutes, racewalking rather than running because of knee and hip injuries. But I endured because I wanted to receive the finishers' medal. More than that, I wanted what that medal represented. I hung in there through a tough race. All the hours spent in training over the previous eighteen months had paid off. That was a great feeling of accomplishment.

But as good as it was, it doesn't hold a candle to the approval and praise of the Lord Jesus Christ that awaits the believer who finishes the race of life faithfully serving his Savior.

Would I have finished that marathon within the six-hour time limit had I not trained for it? I don't think so. Twenty-six miles is a long way! Knowing that the day was coming motivated me to train to be ready for the challenge.

The reality of the coming Judgment Seat of Christ provides a powerful motivation to endure. That is why it is so sad that the vast majority of people sitting in churches every Sunday know little or nothing about the Bema.

It's vital for us as Christians to know that we are accountable. Someday the Lord Jesus will return. And when He does, He will judge us for what we have done during our Christian lives. To borrow a phrase from Dr. Earl Radmacher, "This life is training time for reigning time." How true.

---

[1] It is possible that believers will be observers or even witnesses at the trial of the unsaved. Revelation 20:11-15 discusses the Great White Throne Judgment.

[2] The Bible is not clearer than that on the time of the Bema. It could occur during the Tribulation or during the 75 days between the end of the Tribulation and the start of the Millennium (Daniel 12:11-12). In any case, we will surely experience time differently during the Bema than we do now, for if believers are judged one at a time (which Luke 19:11-26 suggests), each judgment will last only a fraction of a second.

[3] If the blood of Christ covers all our sins, how could the Lord consider any of our bad deeds? See Chapter 5, p. 44, for an answer to that question.

[4] Scripture doesn't contradict itself. The obvious way to harmonize texts that say believers will and won't be judged is to realize that two different types of judgment are in view. The context of John 5:24 is eternal salvation: "He who hears My word and believes in Him who sent Me has everlasting life, and shall not come into judgment, but has passed from death into life." The point is that those who have eternal life will not be judged *at the Great White Throne Judgment* (Revelation 20:11-15). Their eternal destiny is already set (compare John 3:18 and the present tense, "is not condemned"). However, believers will be judged *at the Judgment Seat of Christ* (compare Romans 14:10-12 and 2 Corinthians 5:9-10). The purpose of that judgment is to determine degrees of reward, not eternal destiny.

[5] Zane C. Hodges, *The Epistle of James: Proven Character Through Testing* (Irving, TX: Grace Evangelical Society, 1994), 111-12, emphasis his.

— Chapter 15 —

REMEMBER YOUR INHERITANCE
Galatians 5:19-21

On April 9, 1994, Marie S. Georgeoff died at the age of ninety, leaving one-third of her estate to each of her surviving sons, Edward and Donald, and the children of her deceased son, Thomas. According to the January 3, 2001 issue of the *Akron Beacon Journal,* Donald, the executor of the estate, claimed that his mother's estate was worth only $6,500, the value of a vacant lot she owned.

Thomas's children filed suit, alleging that the estate was worth well over $1 million, nearly all of it in cash. The children remembered that their grandparents, who had made a fortune with a restaurant, bar, and gambling parlor in Akron, kept boxes of cash in their home.

It made a big difference to Thomas's children whether they split one-third of $6,500 or one-third of a million dollars. They were convinced that Donald and his family were hiding their grandmother's money.

We have all heard stories like this, where one relative alleg-edly takes most of the inheritance, in violation of the will.

While no one can take away our God-given inheritance, we *can* forfeit it by the way we live. How much we will receive depends on how we live our Christian lives. To receive the ulti-mate inheritance—ruling with Christ—we must persevere in faith and good works.

On three occasions the apostle Paul listed various vices, warn-ing that people who live like that "will not inherit the kingdom of God" (1 Corinthians 6:9-11; Galatians 5:19-21; and Ephesians 5:5-7). I have chosen Galatians 5:19-21 as the representative text:

> *Now the works of the flesh are evident, which are: adultery, fornication, uncleanness, licentiousness, idolatry, sorcery, hatred, contentions, jealousies, out-bursts of wrath, selfish ambitions, dissensions, her-esies, envy, murders, drunkenness, revelries, and the like; of which I tell you beforehand, just as I also told you in time past, that those who practice such things will not inherit the kingdom of God.*

— What's Going on Here? —

Could this be the same apostle Paul who wrote, "By grace you have been saved through faith, and that not of yourselves; it is the gift of God, not of works, lest anyone should boast" (Ephesians 2:8-9)? And also, "Not by works of righteousness which we have done, but according to His mercy He saved us" (Titus 3:5)? And again, "Now to him who works, the wages are not counted as grace but as debt. But to him who does not work but believes on Him who justifies the ungodly, his faith is accounted for righteousness" (Romans 4:4-5)?

Recognizing the tension here, commentators find various ways to harmonize these passages. Let's examine a few.

Good Works Required to Stay Saved

Those who believe that eternal life can be lost argue that while *initial* salvation is by grace through faith, *final* salvation requires ongoing good works. In other words, the gift is taken back if the recipient doesn't remain worthy of it.

This view is not a harmonization at all because it contradicts the many places in which Paul speaks of justification as apart from works. Paul is not referring merely to pre-salvation works, but to works, period. Notice that if any works are the cause of our salvation, then we have grounds for boasting, and God is indebted to us. Yet Paul says that conclusion cannot be true.

Good Works Required to Prove One Is Saved

Another effort at solving this dilemma comes from Reformed theology, which suggests that all *true* Christians persevere in faith and good works. Thus no *genuine* believer could die as an immoral man, an alcoholic, or even as a jealous or angry man, since those character traits are on the vice lists as well.

The problem with this view is that it still makes good works a condition of getting into the kingdom and fails to harmonize the passages. If you got into the kingdom because you persevered in good works, and another person didn't because he failed to, you would have grounds for boasting and God would be your debtor.

Of course, Reformed theology has an answer for this. It says that it is God who accomplishes the works. Thus they are really *His* works, not *our* works. This sounds good. Yet when asked why there is a passage like this one that, in their opinion, threatens believers with hell, their response is that God uses the threats to motivate us to strive to do good works.

Say what? If they are God's works, then *He* does them. We wouldn't need to cooperate at all. There would be no striving, no need of threats. God is surely powerful enough to make sure we persevere, if that is what He guarantees we will do.

However, God doesn't do this. Unless the believer cooperates with the work of the Holy Spirit, perseverance will not occur.

Besides, there really is no difference between losing your salvation and proving you weren't saved in the first place. You end up in hell either way. Both views make perseverance in good works a requirement of getting into the kingdom—which directly contradicts Paul elsewhere in Scripture.

Assurance is based solely on the promises of the Lord that all who simply believe in Him have everlasting life. No strings attached.

REMEMBER YOUR INHERITANCE

Good Works Required for Inheritance

Here is a simple solution that harmonizes the passages. *Entrance* into the kingdom is attained by grace through faith, apart from works. Yet Paul is warning believers that they will not *inherit* the kingdom if they indulge in wickedness. *Entrance* and *inheritance* are two separate issues.

The Scriptures speak of two types of inheritance for the believer. The first is what I call *passive inheritance.* All believers inherit many things simply because they are children of God.

Second is what I call *active inheritance.* Only those believers who persevere in faith and good works will inherit these things: rulership with Christ, His approval, and the right to wear special white garments, to mention just a few.

In Galatians 5:19-21, *inheriting the kingdom* refers to *active inheritance.* Compare 1 Corinthians 9:24-27, where Paul fears he would not be approved. Or 2 Timothy 2:12, where he warns that only those who endure will reign with Christ. Or Galatians 6:7-9, where he says that only those who sow to the Spirit will reap a full experience of eternal life.

One passage in which both types of inheritance can be easily seen together is Romans 8:16-17. It reads:

> *The Spirit Himself bears witness with our spirit that we are children of God, and if children, then heirs—heirs of God and joint heirs with Christ, if indeed we suffer with Him, that we may also be glorified together.*

- 129 -

All believers are passive heirs because they are children of God. There are things that they have now and will have forever, no matter what they do. These include four ministries of the Holy Spirit which occur at the moment we first believe in Christ for eternal life. I remember these ministries with the acronym RIBS. The Spirit regenerates, indwells, baptizes (into the Body of Christ), and seals us the moment we believe in Jesus.

Other aspects of passive inheritance are citizenship in God's kingdom and future resurrection with glorified bodies. None of these things are dependent on our perseverance. They are thus things we *passively* inherit.

However, there is a type of inheritance that is limited to those believers who persevere in their service for Christ. Those believers who live for Christ and hence "suffer with Him" will be "joint heirs with Christ" and will also be "glorified together" with Him. This co-heirship and co-glorification includes ruling with Christ forever. Only those believers who persevere in self-sacrificing service for Christ will receive this active type of inheritance.

Don't forget about your inheritance. While you can't lose eternal life, you *can* fail to inherit the kingdom. Like the Prodigal Son, as long as we are in the spiritual far country, we are not in fellowship with the Father and we have squandered our inheritance. Willful rebellion against the Lord will result in forfeiture of the right to reign with Christ. Only when we return to fellowship with Him can we once again be in line to inherit.

— Chapter 16 —

WALK WITHOUT STUMBLING
Jude 24

One of the greatest fears many churchgoers have is that they will fall away from the Lord and either lose their salvation or prove that they weren't really saved in the first place.

The net effect of these two fears is the same: A lack of assurance that is terrifying. What an awful way to go through life.

We should fear falling away from the Lord—not because we will end up in hell, for believers are eternally secure (John 11:26)—but because our fullness of life in eternity is directly related to our perseverance in the faith now.

Jude 24 concerns the problem of falling away and its associated loss of joy. As he closes his epistle, Jude writes:

> *Now to Him who is able to keep you from stumbling, And to present you faultless Before the presence of His glory with exceeding joy ...*
> —Jude 24

God is able to keep every believer from stumbling, that is, from experiencing major moral or doctrinal failure. A key question here is whether Jude was conveying *an unconditional guarantee* that God will keep all believers from stumbling or whether he was referring to *a conditional guarantee* that requires a certain response by believers.

Both in light of Scripture and experience, the idea that this is an unconditional guarantee is impossible. We need only to think of saints like David, Solomon, Peter, John Mark, and Demas—all of whom stumbled badly.

Nevertheless, a number of pastors and theologians suggest that Jude 24 *is* an unconditional promise.[1] One author uses Jude 24 in an effort to prove his contention that, "God will keep His own [from apostasy]."[2] Another cites Jude 24 as proof "of the perseverance of God in protecting and preserving His people in faith."[3]

I believe that many commentators have missed the mark in explaining this text. Jude 24 *calls* for perseverance, but does not *guarantee* it. Furthermore, it is not dealing with eternal security at all.

— Ability Is Not a Guarantee —

Nothing bad that happens is outside of God's control. Take, for example, the Fall of Adam and Eve. God could have created our first parents without the ability to sin, but He didn't. He could have kept the serpent from tempting them, but He didn't.

Consider three examples where the expressions *God is able*, *He is able*, and *I am able* (where Jesus is the speaker) are used. In each, the possible result either never occurred or it occurred only when a condition was met.

(1) John the Baptist said, *"God is able* to raise up children to Abraham from these stones"* (Matthew 3:9, emphasis mine). He was able to do that, but He never did.

(2) The author of Hebrews wrote, *"He is able* to aid those who are tempted"* (Hebrews 2:18, emphasis mine). While God is able to aid those who are tempted, the author of Hebrews indicates that this aid is conditioned upon the one being tempted looking to Him in prayer with faith (Hebrews 3:12-15; 4:11-16). Hebrews 2:18 is in no way a blanket promise that God will aid all who are tempted. The Christian who is away from God and who isn't praying for God's help will find that he is unable, in his own strength, to successfully meet the challenges of the temptations that come.

(3) Similarly, in Matthew 9:28, Jesus conditioned the healing of two blind men upon their answer to this question, "Do you believe *that I am able* to do this?" (emphasis mine).

The fact that God is *able* to do something doesn't unconditionally guarantee that He *will* do it. It may be something He never intends to do. Or He may do it only for those who respond as He commands, as is the case in Jude 24.

— To Keep You from Stumbling —

This is the only New Testament occurrence of the word translated here as "stumble," and it refers to *losing one's footing, stumbling,* or *falling.* Clearly its use is figurative. Some suggest that only doctrinal slippage is meant, but Jude was warning his readers about false teachers who were promoting *both* false doctrine *and* licentious living (see verses 15-18).

Jude was encouraging believers to look to the One who can keep them from being duped by false teachers (note verses 20-23). To suggest that in verse 24 Jude was unconditionally guaranteeing his readers that they wouldn't be duped is to destroy the whole point of the letter! It was Jude's fear that the false teachers *would* dupe his readers that prompted him to write this letter (see verses 3-4).

— To Present You Faultless with Joy —

Many commentators take the position that God *guarantees* freedom from stumbling because they conclude from the use of the word *faultless* that eternal salvation must be in view.

One author writes,

> But pursue it [sanctification] we will if we are truly born again, for God Himself guarantees our perseverance in righteousness...He is able to keep you from stumbling, and to make you stand in the presence of His glory blameless with great joy (Jude 24).[4]

Another author relates verse 24 back to verse 21 and says,

> It is noteworthy that when Jude exhorts us to keep ourselves in the love of God (v. 21), he concludes with a doxology for Him who is able to keep us from falling and who will present us without blemish before the presence of His glory (v. 24). The warning passages are *means* which God uses in our life to accomplish His purpose in grace.[5]

However, eternal life is eternal. The Lord Jesus promised that once anyone ate of the bread of life he would *never hunger again* (John 6:35). Once anyone drank the water of life, he would *never thirst again* (John 6:35). Never means never. The believer who falls remains eternally secure. Why? Because God guarantees it! The moment we come to faith, our eternal salvation is *FDIC* insured: *Father's Declaration Is Certain.*

Jude is talking instead about the future judgment of believers at the Judgment Seat of Christ where the Lord Jesus will present every believer before the Father. But not all believers will be presented as "faultless," nor will all believers have "exceeding joy" at the Bema. Only those believers who have persevered will have such an experience. Compare Matthew 16:27; Mark 8:38; 1 Corinthians 9:27; 2 Corinthians 5:10; and 1 John 2:28.

The word "faultless" *(amomos)* means "without spot" or "without blemish." Sometimes it is used to mean complete sinlessness, as when it is used in reference to the Lord Jesus (see Hebrews 9:14; 1 Peter 1:19). However, it can also refer to an experience which, though not sinless, is nevertheless pleasing to God, because it reflects faithfulness to Him. For example, Revelation 14:5 speaks of 144,000 Jewish evangelists during the Tribulation, "In their mouth was found no guile, for they are *without fault* [*amomos*] before the throne of God." Compare also Colossians 1:22 and 2 Peter 3:14.

The same idea, though using a different Greek word (*anenkletos*), is found in the requirements for elders in the church. Elders and deacons are men who must be "blameless" in their experience (1 Timothy 3:10; Titus 1:6-7). Likewise, Elizabeth and Zacharias were said to be "blameless" (*amemptoi*) in their experience (Luke 1:6).

God rewards faithfulness. A special measure of joy at the Judgment Seat of Christ and forever thereafter is waiting for believers who do not lose their footing.

— We Can't Blame God —

Comedian Flip Wilson used to quip, "The devil made me do it." But for Christians at the Judgment Seat of Christ, no excuses will be valid. We won't be able to legitimately blame the devil, our parents, our spouses, our children, our genes, illness, society, circumstances, or God Himself.[6] Nothing can "make us" stumble from the path of righteousness. If any of us walks away from God, we do so because we have failed to look to Him who is able to keep us from stumbling (cf. Romans 16:25; 2 Peter 3:14-18).

Victory is possible in the Christian life because God is ready, willing, and *able* to sustain us through the temptations and trials we face. The question is not whether He is able to keep us from stumbling. Rather, the question is, whether we will continue to look in faith and obedience to Him who *is* able to keep us from stumbling.

----

[1] See, for example, Edward C. Pentecost, "Jude," in *The Bible Knowledge Commentary*, New Testament edition (Wheaton: Victor Books, 1983), 2:923-24; Edwin A. Blum, "Jude," in the *Zondervan NIV Bible Commentary*, Vol. 2, New Testament (Grand Rapids: Zondervan Publishing House, 1994), 1124; Michael Green, *The Second Epistle of Peter and the Epistle of Jude,* Tyndale New Testament Commentaries (Grand Rapids: Wm. B. Eerdmans Publishing Company, 1968), 189-91. Also see notes 2 and 3 below.

[2] John F. MacArthur, Jr., *The Gospel According to Jesus: What Does Jesus Mean When He Says, "Follow Me"?*, revised and expanded edition (Grand Rapids: Zondervan Publishing House, 1988, 1994), 105. See also n. 7 on page 106 where he says that 2 Timothy 2:19 "underscores the truth that saving faith, which is wrought by God, cannot fail. We cannot always see whose faith is genuine and whose is a sham, but God knows."

[3] Donald S. Whitney, *How Can I Be Sure I'm a Christian?: What the Bible Says About Assurance of Salvation* (Colorado Springs: NavPress Publishing Group, 1994), 29.

[4] John F. MacArthur, Jr., *Faith Works: The Gospel According to the Apostles* (Dallas, TX: Word Publishers, 1993), 130. See also his comments about Jude 24 on 180, 185.

[5] Charles Horne, *Salvation* (Chicago: Moody Press, 1971), 95. Note that staying in God's love is equated with getting into the kingdom. Why couldn't Jude be saying instead that believers continue to experience God's love only as long as they persevere? Believers experience God's wrath when they fall away (Romans 13:4-5; Ephesians 5:6-7; Hebrews 3:11; 4:3).

⁶ This is not to suggest that the Lord Jesus will fail to take these things into account at His Judgment Seat. We will each be evaluated according to our own ability (Matthew 25:15; Luke 12:48; 1 Corinthians 4:1-5). None of us begins the Christian life at precisely the same place morally. Nor do we have the same spiritual gifts, talents, treasure, and opportunity. The Lord will take all of this into account. The point here is that none of these things are excuses for falling away from the Lord. The Lord will keep every Christian who is walking in fellowship with Him from falling away.

— Chapter 17 —

KEEP YOUR EYES ON THE PRIZE
1 Corinthians 9:24-27

"I really cannot give you the formula for success. But I can give you the formula for failure: Try to please everyone." That saying by an unknown sage is so true. If you try to please everyone, you are destined to fail.

Studies show that about one in five people you meet don't like you even before you've said anything. They may decide this based simply on your size, shape, color, race, religion, or clothing. Many of them cannot be won over, no matter what you say.

In his famous song "Garden Party," Rick Nelson sang in the climactic last line, "You see, you can't please everyone, so you got to please yourself." Many people feel that way today. Realizing they can't have everyone's approval, they turn to hedonism, whatever makes them feel good.

Most of us admit to having a strong desire for the approval of at least those closest to us. While we can't please all people, we surely want to please the most important people in our lives. At work we want to know that our employers approve of us. That affects how we feel about our job, and whether we receive raises and promotions. Everyone wants the approval of a spouse, for, lacking that, each day becomes a trial.

Parental approval is paramount, because apart from a spouse, no other human's approval means as much as Mom's and Dad's. Studies show that many adults are still trying to please their parents. In fact, even after Mom and Dad have died, many adults continue to long for that approval.

However, God's approval is the most important approval anyone can have. After all, He is our Creator, the One to whom we are accountable (Hebrews 4:13). As Christians, we will be judged by the Lord Jesus. His approval is something every Christian should strive to gain and maintain.

Assurance of salvation—knowing for sure that you have eternal life and can never lose it—is a vital part of the Christian life. Such assurance produces gratitude and motivates obedience.

Yet many passages, including 1 Corinthians 9:24-27, suggest that if we fail to persevere as believers, we will miss out on something. In this case, that which is potentially forfeited is God's approval. What we are in danger of missing is not the kingdom, but rewards once we get there. While eternal life can't be lost, eternal rewards can be.

— Paul Was Sure of His Eternal Destiny —

For the many Bible interpreters who do not believe it is possible to be sure that you will enter the kingdom, the idea of seeking God's approval is a salvation issue. Some commentators understand Paul to be expressing doubts in the following passage, about whether or not he would make it to heaven!

> *Do you not know that those who run in a race all run, but one receives the prize? Run in such a way that you may obtain it. And everyone who competes for the prize is temperate in all things. Now they do it to obtain a perishable crown, but we for an imperishable crown. Therefore I run thus: not with uncertainty. Thus I fight: not as one who beats the air. But I discipline my body and bring it into subjection, lest, when I have preached to others, I myself should become disqualified.*
> —1 Corinthians 9:24-27

Many believe that Paul was here expressing fear that he might lose eternal life.[1] Others say he feared he might prove he never really *had* eternal life.[2]

Such suggestions concern me. For if the apostle Paul wasn't sure he was eternally secure, then who *can* be sure? Whether Calvinist or Arminian, such thinking is what I call "daisy theology."

Daisy theology is the view that we can't be sure of our eternal destiny until we die. Remember the young girl plucking off the petals of a daisy? As she pulled off each petal she'd say alternately,

"He loves me. He loves me not." She hoped that the one left at the end would be the "He loves me" petal. Sadly, many Christians live like that. They hope that when the sands of their hourglass run out, God will love them and give them entrance into the kingdom.

But didn't Paul elsewhere indicate that he was absolutely certain he was eternally secure (e.g., Romans 8:38-39; Ephesians 2:8-9; 1 Timothy 1:16; 2 Timothy 1:12)? Commentators who think Paul expressed doubts in 1 Corinthians 9:24-27 call this "a tension."[3] I'll say. This type of thinking gives me a tension headache!

Most in Christendom believe that no one can be sure before he dies that he will get into the kingdom. The reason is that any one of us could fail to persevere.

I don't know if I can say strongly enough how much this view of "assurance" grieves me. Of course, the idea that we must persevere to get into the kingdom not only destroys assurance, but it destroys the good news as well. In most churches today, pastors across denominational lines, are teaching that perseverance is a condition of entering the kingdom. Unfortunately this is also true of the vast majority of seminary and Bible college professors. That is doubly sad because they are training the *next* generation of pastors and teachers. This trend will only increase unless the Lord raises up concerned individuals to proclaim the truth with love and conviction.

Leon Morris holds to the Reformed Doctrine of the Perseverance of the Saints—the belief that all genuine Christians will persevere in faith and good works. Thus it is especially significant that he does not see assurance in view in this passage. Commenting on 1 Corinthians 9:27, Morris said:

> Paul's fear was not that he might lose his salvation, but that he might suffer loss *through failing to satisfy his Lord* (cf. 3:15).[4]

He had this to say about 1 Corinthians 3:15:

> *He will suffer loss* means he will lose his wage, a workman fined for poor workmanship. Being saved "as through fire" (RSV) may have been a proverbial expression to indicate one is saved and no more.[5]

Paul had eternal life and knew it. He didn't fear he might not make it into the kingdom. And neither should any of us who believe in Christ. It is impossible for one who believes in Christ to fail to make it into the kingdom, for God guarantees it, whether we persevere or not (John 6:35-40; 11:25-27).

Eternal salvation is a gift—not a prize to be won for work done.

— Perseverance Required for the Prize —

The imagery Paul presents in 1 Corinthians 9:24-27 is that of athletic competition. Possibly Paul was thinking specifically of the Isthmian Games, athletic contests held every two years near Corinth. They were similar to the Olympics of today, and included running and boxing events.

In athletic events such as these, all participants are part of the competition, but only one wins. In that day the prize was a pine wreath.[6]

In Christian competition, believers work *with*, not against, each other. *All* can win in the Christian life. In fact, the more we help each other, the more we will all win. The prize for which we Christians strive is imperishable. It will never fade away or be destroyed by time or death. It is eternal.

I ran track during high school and college. In 1995 when I turned forty-three, I decided to take up the sport again. After joining the Master's division of the U. S. Track and Field Association, I competed in races in and around the Dallas area. What a joy it was to run fast again and even to win a medal on occasion! However, as impressive as the medals are to look at, they are only a temporary pleasure.

Paul knew that Christ approved of him (see 1 Corinthians 3:5-9; 4:1, 11-13, 16; 9:1-23; 11:1)[7] because he knew he was faithfully serving Him. But would he maintain Christ's approval to the end of his life? Paul could not be sure, for he knew he had to persevere to retain that approval. And he knew that no Christian, not even he himself, could be sure he would persevere.

— The Prize for Perseverance —

The Lord Jesus will give an imperishable crown to those believers whom He approves. Elsewhere Paul said, "If we endure, we shall also reign with Him" (2 Timothy 2:12a). Ruling with Christ is a privilege every believer should desire. It should motivate us to persevere in a life of faith. Paul had his eyes on the prize. Do you?

— Conclusion —

Alfred Rascon was an Army Medic in Vietnam on March 16, 1966, when his unit came under fire so intense that Rascon later called it "ten minutes of pure hell." While helping a fatally wounded machine gunner, Rascon took a bullet in the back that nearly penetrated his spine. He had good reason to quit and wait for medical evacuation. But he could still move, so he pressed on. Under heavy fire, Rascon took ammunition to another machine gunner. While delivering the ammo, a grenade went off at his feet and he was hit in the head, wounding him in the mouth, nose, and ears. He certainly had every reason to quit now.

When another grenade landed, Rascon fell on a fellow soldier, absorbing the blow. Surely now he would quit. He got up and saw another grenade land near his wounded staff sergeant. Again Rascon fell on his comrade and took the shrapnel himself.

At this point he could barely walk. Yet he had no give-up in him. On he went.

"And then," said President Bill Clinton in his February 8, 2000 Congressional Medal of Honor award ceremony at the White House, "barely able to walk, bleeding from his ears and nose, he ran to recover a machine gun that the enemy was about to capture. The extra firepower kept the enemy from advancing, and Alfred Rascon saved his platoon."

Time and time again Alfred could have given up. But with the strength he had left, he kept risking his life to save others. He was responsible for saving many men in his platoon, if not the entire platoon, as the President's remarks suggested.

Amazingly, Rascon recovered from his wounds and not only completed that tour in Vietnam, but served a second tour as well. He remained in the Army until 1976. Since that time he has continued in government service.

Am I that committed in my service for the Lord Jesus Christ? Is there give-up in me? Or am I in this for the long haul? We need to ask ourselves these questions. The Lord Jesus may well return any day now. But if He should tarry for several decades, will we persevere?

God places a premium on ending well. It is important that we persevere in our service for Christ. Quitters will not receive His approval. While eternal life is received the moment we believe in Christ and is secure forever, approval is received only by putting our faith to work. Approval can be lost. Our aim should be to maintain a standing of full approval, maximizing our lives for Christ so that we will hear those blessed words, "Well done, good and faithful servant."

---

[1] Concerning 1 Corinthians 9:24-27, Gordon Fee writes: "[Paul] 'disciplined' himself 'for the sake of the gospel,' *so that he, along with them, might share in the promises of the gospel*...But does Paul actually mean that one can fail to obtain the prize? Some would say no, but usually because of a prior theological

commitment, not because of what the text itself says...*It would be sheer folly to suggest that the warnings are not real. Paul keeps warning and assurance in tension.* Simultaneously he *exhorts* and, by this and the following examples, *warns* the Corinthians of their imminent danger if they do not exercise 'self control' in the matter of idolatry..." (*The First Epistle to the Corinthians,* New International Commentary Series [Grand Rapids: Wm. B. Eerdmans Publishing Company, 1987], 439-40, italics mine).

[2] Charles Hodge wrote concerning verse 27: "He made these strenuous exertions, lest, having preached the gospel to others, he himself should become (*adokimos*) a reprobate, one rejected. What an argument and what a reproof is this! The reckless and listless Corinthians thought they could safely indulge themselves to the very verge of sin, *while this devoted apostle considered himself as engaged in a life-struggle for his salvation*" (*Commentary on the First Epistle to the Corinthians* [Grand Rapids: Wm. B. Eerdmans Publishing Company, Reprinted 1980], 169, italics mine).

Yet Hodge goes on to point to Romans 8:38-39 and to say that Paul not only expressed fears, but also "the most joyful assurance of salvation" (169). How are doubts and assurance harmonized in one mind? He suggests that, "the one state of mind is the necessary condition of the other. It is only those who are conscious of this constant and deadly struggle with sin, to whom this assurance is given" (169).

See also *The New Geneva Study Bible: Bringing the Light of the Reformation to Scripture* (Nashville: Thomas Nelson Publishers, 1995), 1811. A note indicates: "It would be wrong to dismiss or minimize Paul's concern (cf. 15:2; Phil. 3:11; Col. 1:23) by suggesting that it is merely hypothetical or relates only to rewards and not salvation. Paul was confident that absolutely nothing would be able to separate him from God's love (Rom. 8:38-39), *but he never presumed that he was saved regardless of what he did.* No Christian can afford to take lightly the warnings of Scripture (10:12)" (emphasis mine).

[3] In essence they are saying that assurance is trumped by warnings.

[4] Leon Morris, *1 Corinthians,* revised edition, Tyndale New Testament Commentaries (Grand Rapids: Wm. B. Eerdmans Publishing Company, 1958, 1985), 138, italics mine.

[5] Ibid., 66, italics his.

[6] Professor Oscar Broneer, Director of the American School of Archaeology, says: "The prize of victory at Isthmia was a wreath, at first made of pine, but in the fifth century B.C. a wreath of wild celery was introduced. In late Hellenistic times and in the Roman era, both types of wreaths were awarded to victors in the Games. The celery of the Isthmian crown was withered, in contrast to the

Nemean which was made of fresh celery. The withered wreath bestowed upon winners at Isthmia may have lent color to the Apostle Paul's statement in his first Epistle to the Corinthians (9.25), where he contrasts the 'imperishable wreath' ('incorruptible crown' in the King James version), which the Christians receive, with the 'perishable wreath' of the athletes. Paul may well have been at Isthmus for the celebration of the Games in the year 51, when he lived and worked as tent-maker in Corinth." See http://www.ioa.leeds.ac.uk/1970s/70094.htm.

[7] It is true that nowhere does Paul specifically use the term *approved* in any of these verses. However, the concept is clearly present in those texts. It is instructive to compare Romans 16:10 where Paul says of a member of the Church of Rome: "Greet Apelles, *approved* in Christ" (emphasis mine). He does not say *Greet Apelles who will be approved if he perseveres*. No, he speaks of him as being an approved Christian worker at the time of the writing of the epistle. Surely if he called one who worked under him "approved in Christ" he knew himself to be approved as well. However, as the case of Demas shows (compare Colossians 4:14; Philemon 24; and 2 Timothy 4:10), one who is an approved workman may forfeit that status. See my article "Demas Has Forsaken Me," available at http://www.faithalone.org/news/y1995/95jan2.html.

~ Section 5 ~

APPENDICES

If, after reading
The Road to Reward,
you still have questions,
the following appendices
have been written
with you in mind.

— Appendix 1 —

WON'T ALL BELIEVERS
BE EQUALLY REWARDED?
Matthew 20:1-16

A leading New Testament scholar writes concerning the Parable of the Day Laborers (Matthew 20:1-16): "Almost everyone agrees that Jesus is teaching about a fundamental equality here among those who are truly his disciples. All are rewarded alike."[1]

Let's take a minute to review the particulars of this parable:

> • Early one morning a landowner hired a group of laborers to work in his vineyard all day for one denarius each.

> • At 9:00 a.m. he chose another group to go work and told them he would pay them whatever was right.

> • Again he went out at about noon and 3:00 p.m., and hired two more groups.

• At about 5:00 p.m. he went out and found another group that no one had hired. He sent them to the vineyard, and promised to pay them whatever was right.

• At the end of the day, when it was time to pay the workers, he paid those who only worked one hour one denarius each.

• When the first group came, they expected to receive more, even though they had agreed to work for one denarius. "They complained against the landowner, saying 'These last men have worked only one hour, and you made them equal to us who have borne the burden and the heat of the day.'"

• The landowner's response was, "Friend, I am doing you no wrong. Did you not agree with me for a denarius? Take what is yours and go your way. I wish to give this last man the same as to you. Is it not lawful for me to do what I wish with my own things? Or is your eye evil because I am good?"

This parable does seem to teach that everyone will be equally rewarded. However, we know from many other texts discussed previously in this book that this is not the case. The real lesson of the parable is that those believers *who have served Him faithfully for their entire Christian lives,* will be rewarded equally *regardless of the length of their Christian lives.*

All five groups represent believers who heed the call of discipleship from the start of their Christian experience. That is evident by the fact that as soon as they were hired, they all went to work. What distinguishes their length of service is how long they were Christians before death or the Rapture.

The length of time one is born again prior to death or the Rapture is not a limiting factor in how he will be rewarded.[2] The person who served Christ faithfully for the *one year* he was a Christian will be equally rewarded with someone who served Christ for *eighty years*. Of course, this assumes both people served the Lord wholeheartedly during that time. (Admittedly that is a variable the Lord does not discuss in this parable.) The Lord can and will extrapolate what we would have done if we had had more time.

When I was on staff with Campus Crusade for Christ, we were seeking to fulfill the Great Commission in the U.S. by the end of 1976 and in the world by the end of 1980. In 1977 when I was considering leaving staff to attend seminary, I remember expressing my concern to Josh McDowell that I didn't want to miss out on ministry while I prepared to minister. But I really believed I would be able to serve the Lord more effectively if I had a theological education. I felt torn.

His response to me was that there would always be people to win for Christ. And that I should go to seminary.

Later while in seminary a student asked one of our professors what would happen if the Rapture occurred while we were in seminary. Wouldn't we miss out on rewards over those who chose to keep on ministering without seminary?

"No, you wouldn't," said the professor. "There surely will be many in seminary at the time of the Rapture. That doesn't mean that preparation is unwise. We all are to do our best in serving Christ. For some that includes special training for ministry. Should the Lord come when you are in school, He will take into account not only what you have done, but what you have prepared to do. He knows what you would have done had you had a full life."

The Parable of the Day Laborers in Matthew 20 is not an invitation to start serving Christ whenever we feel like it. Rather, it is an encouragement that no matter how long it is between our new birth and the time we go to be with the Lord, He will reward us fairly. We need not dread the Rapture as though it could snatch away our opportunity to rule with Christ and to have treasure in heaven. Be faithful and follow Christ. He will reward us fairly.

---

[1] Craig L. Blomberg, "Degrees of Reward in the Kingdom of Heaven?" *Journal of the Evangelical Theological Society* (June 1992):160.

[2] Note that I didn't say that the length of time one *serves* is not a limiting factor in how much we are rewarded. For length of service may well be a limiting factor in rewards. The person who was a Christian for thirty years but only served for the last ten would not be as highly rewarded as one who served Christ faithfully his entire Christian life (however long that was). Only in cases where length of service coincides with length of time one is a believer is length of service not a limiting factor.

— Appendix 2 —

WON'T THIS LEAD TO JEALOUSY IN THE KINGDOM?

Children have a very hard time with jealousy. "He got more ice cream than I did!" "I want a bike like Suzy got for her birthday!" The more we mature, of course, the less jealousy we should experience; but to one degree or another, jealousy is a problem for all of us.

One question that I have heard repeatedly as I have taught on rewards is, "If some will have more than others in the kingdom, won't this lead to jealousy?"

— Jealousy Is Sin —

Jealousy is sin. Since we know that there won't be any sin in the kingdom, we are faced with two possible answers to our question: (1) All will have exactly the same possessions, honor, power, and experience in the kingdom, or, (2) While possessions, honor, power, and experience will vary, no one will be jealous.

For the first possibility to be accurate, the following would have to be true:

> *Major premise:* Some having more than others *always* results in jealousy.
>
> *Minor premise:* There will be no jealousy in the kingdom.
>
> *Conclusion:* Therefore, no one will have more than others in the kingdom.

Though this might seem logical, we know the conclusion is wrong, based on the many Scripture passages discussed in this book. If the conclusion is in error, then something is wrong with either the major or minor premise.

Since there will be no sin, and hence no jealousy in the kingdom, the minor premise is correct. That leaves the major premise with a problem.

Even in this life, the fact that some have more than others doesn't *necessarily* result in jealousy. A mature believer is content with what he or she has and is not jealous of another person having a better car, home, or whatever. Surely the major premise was not true of the apostle Paul.

Jealousy exists now to varying degrees in both unbelievers and believers. However, it will not exist at all in the eternal kingdom of the Lord Jesus Christ. Glorified saints will never be jealous because they will never sin. Contentment will be their hallmark forever. So we should look at the matter of jealousy in this way:

Major premise: Some having more than others *sometimes* results in jealousy now.

Minor premise: There will be no jealousy in the kingdom.

Conclusion: Some having more than others *will never* result in jealousy then.

— Will We Be Jealous of Jesus? —

It should be obvious that the Lord Jesus will have more reward than anyone else in the kingdom. After all, He is the King of kings and Lord of lords who will rule over the entire world. The wealth of the universe will be His. Does that mean some might be jealous of Him? Hardly! Remember, if degrees of honor, glory, possessions, and power necessarily result in jealousy, then we would all be forever jealous of the Lord Jesus!

Based on the writings of Ezekiel, many believe that David will be prince forever over the nation of Israel. That means he will be Jesus' right-hand man in the rulership over Israel.

We also know from the Gospels that the apostles will sit on twelve thrones and rule over the twelve tribes of Israel. Evidently they will serve under the direction of David. Thus David will have more authority than they will and they will have more authority than the citizens of Israel over whom they rule.

Yet no one will be jealous of David or the apostles or a host of others who have earned the right to these exalted positions.

— No Jealousy, No Sin —

We need to realize that in the kingdom we will be free from what Paul calls *the flesh*. While they will be real, our glorified bodies will be immortal and incapable of sinning.

Even though Augustine was not always clear on the gospel, what he had to say 1,500 years ago on the subject of degrees of reward and potential envy is worth heeding:

> But who can conceive, not to say describe, what degrees of honour and glory shall be awarded to the various degrees of merit? Yet it cannot be doubted that there shall be degrees. And in that blessed city there shall be this great blessing, that no inferior shall envy any superior, as now the archangels are not envied by the angels, because no one will wish to be what he has not received, though bound in the strictest concord with him who has received; as in the body the finger does not seek to be the eye, though both members are harmoniously included in the complete structure of the body. And thus, along with his gift, greater or less, each shall receive this further gift of contentment to desire no more than he has.[1]

Everyone in the eternal kingdom will certainly be content. However, there is a sense in which we might feel regret if we fail to rule with Christ, or if we rule to a much lesser degree than we might have because we squandered our chance to do more for Him during our lifetime.

So, we dare not slough off the idea of rewards on the grounds that it will result in jealousy. As we say here in Texas, "That dog won't hunt." Rather than looking for an excuse not to do our best for Christ, let's get busy and work hard for Him (2 Timothy 2:6). We'll be forever glad if we do.

---

[1] Augustine, *The City of God*, Bk. 22.30.

— Appendix 3 —

WHAT WILL ETERNITY BE LIKE?

Are you prepared for eternity? Do the words of the apostle Paul resonate within you "...to live is Christ and to die is gain" (Philippians 1:21)? Do you wonder what life after death will be like? Christians don't need to wonder, for God has already told us what eternity will be like.

Even so, I've found that for most Christians, eternity is an abstract concept. They seem to think that this life is much more exciting and enjoyable than eternity will be. However, once we gain a clear picture of what eternity will be like, it has a profound effect on how we live now.

Once we die, there won't be another chance for us to prepare for eternity. Hebrews 9:27 tells us that "it is appointed for men to die once, but after this the judgment." That is why it is vital that we prepare *now* for eternity because after we die it will be too late.

I'd like for you to take a five-question exam on eternity. If you can answer these questions well, you have a good start on preparing for eternity.

— Where Do You Plan to Spend Eternity? —

Many believers think that heaven will be their eternal home. This may come as a surprise, but the Bible teaches that no one will spend eternity in heaven. The Bible *does* say that when Christians die they go to be with the Lord in heaven. However, the Bible *does not* say that we will spend eternity—up there—in heaven. Revelation 21:1-3 gives us the answer to where we will spend eternity:

> *And I saw a new heaven and a new earth, for the first heaven and the first earth had passed away. Also there was no more sea. Then I, John, saw the holy city, New Jerusalem, coming down out of heaven from God, prepared as a bride adorned for her husband. And I heard a loud voice from heaven saying, "Behold, the tabernacle of God is with men, and He will dwell with them, and they shall be His people, and God Himself will be with them and be their God."*

If you read on in this chapter you will find that there will be twelve literal gates made of pearls—the famous pearly gates. There will be nations, cities, streets, and buildings made of gold, silver, and precious stones.

The new earth will be free from the curse. There will be no pollution, death, or decay. It will be paradise—the Garden of Eden revisited.

Now let's move to the next question.

— What Will You Look Like in Eternity? —

Some believe (I should say, hope), that we will all look the same. All men will look like Mr. Universe and all women will look like Miss Universe.

Well, there's some bad news and some good news.

The bad news is that in eternity we will look a lot like we look now. That means that there will still be tall and short people, thin and husky, basses and tenors, sopranos and altos, introverts and extroverts, etc.

Remember that on the Mount of Transfiguration the Lord Jesus spoke with Moses and Elijah who had been dead for many centuries—yet they looked like they did when they were alive. The same will be true of us as well.

After His resurrection Jesus Christ was recognizable—except on those occasions when God supernaturally kept His identity hidden for a time.

In the account of the rich man and Lazarus in Luke 16, we find that both men were still recognizable after death. So was Abraham.

The good news is that all of our scars, blemishes, deformities, handicaps, and the like will be gone. In eternity we will have glorious bodies with unique appearances and personalities.

Revelation 21:4 tells us that in eternity, "God will wipe away every tear from [our] eyes; there shall be no more death, nor sorrow, nor crying, and there shall be no more pain, for the former things have passed away." I'd say that is good news indeed!

Okay. How are you doing so far on our final exam? Are you ready for our third question?

— What Do You Expect to Do in Eternity? —

The three most popular answers are: sing forever in a big choir, float on the clouds, and hum a lot.

Actually the Bible teaches that we will engage in three activities in eternity. Before I tip my hand as to what these are, consider the Garden of Eden and the nation of Israel when God was her King. What did God instruct Adam and Eve to do? What would eternity have been like if they hadn't sinned? What did God ask the people of Israel to do? What would eternity have been like if the nation of Israel had not rejected God and had received Jesus Christ when He came?

The Garden of Eden and the nation of Israel are models of what eternity will be like.

The first thing we will do in eternity is work. Work is not really a bad word because God made us to enjoy work. The curse has made work less enjoyable than it should be. However, we are created in the image of God and as such are creative beings. It is an inate part of our nature. We enjoy working and producing.

It will be a delight to serve God in His kingdom through our work as artists, poets, architects, engineers, carpenters, farmers, and so forth. There will be a host of jobs to do then—except that a few current jobs will be conspicuously absent, such as undertakers, police, prison guards, and criminals, to name a few.

Second, we will worship. Revelation 21:24 tells us that "the nations of those who are saved shall walk in its light, and the kings of the earth bring their glory and honor into it [the New Jerusalem]."

Worship is often very enjoyable now. However, it will be fantastic in eternity! Imagine listening to Abraham, Moses, Elijah, John the Baptist, Peter, Paul and other great prophets and preachers of the past—indeed even the Lord Jesus Himself. Think of it. We will worship the King of kings and Lord of lords in person!

Third, we will enjoy fellowship and recreation. At the Last Supper the Lord said that He would not drink wine again until He did so with His disciples in the kingdom. There will be fellowship meals and banquets in eternity.

The Lord spoke of mansions in eternity during His Upper Room Discourse.

In the Sermon on the Mount Jesus instructed us to lay up treasures in heaven.

The future will be more glorious than the past as we develop new vehicles, sports, games, books, music, plays, buildings, spacecraft, and who knows what else.

— How Do We Enter God's Kingdom? —

Here are some answers I often hear: pray, read the Bible, attend church faithfully, be good, obey the Golden Rule, be baptized, promise to serve God, and serve God daily.

All of those things are good—but none of them can get anyone into God's kingdom.

We are all sinners. None of us is perfect; but God is. He sent His Son, Jesus Christ, to die on the cross and pay the full and complete payment for all our sins. He is thus able to give eternal life as a gift. To receive it we need do only one thing: believe in Jesus Christ.

Why should God let those who simply believe in Jesus into His kingdom? Because He made a promise and He keeps all His promises. "He who believes in Me has everlasting life" (John 6:47). It's that simple. Merely believe in Him, not in Him plus your works (see John 6:28-29 and Ephesians 2:8-9). And He *must* let you into His kingdom. He guarantees it.

All right. Are you ready for the final question?

— How Can We Fully Enjoy Eternity? —

All the answers that were *incorrect* on the previous question are *correct* here: pray, read the Bible, attend church faithfully, do good works, obey the Golden Rule, be baptized, promise to serve God, and then do so daily.

While entrance into the eternal kingdom is a gift we receive by faith alone, eternal rewards are earned by our faithfulness.

For the Christian, this life is a sort of *proving ground*. It is a time of testing to determine what our role will be in eternity.

All on the new earth will enjoy eternity. However, some will have a much fuller experience than others (2 Timothy 2:12; Revelation 2:7, 17; 3:4; 22:14).

Until we die or are raptured, we are to keep on preparing for eternity. Those who have trusted in Christ, are guaranteed to be in the kingdom, but for the rest of our lives we will be preparing for the quality of experience we will have there.

Only One Life,
T'will Soon Be Past,
Only What's Done For Christ,
Will Last!

— Study Guide —

B ible study is a great way to grow in our faith. The questions in this Study Guide may be used for personal or group study. They are designed to make you think. The chapters provide the background to help you discover the answers.

If you discuss these questions in a group setting, you will surely find differences of opinion. Let those differences move you to look carefully at the Word of God, where the answers are to be found.

May we all be like the Bereans who searched the Scriptures daily to see if the things spoken by Paul and Silas were true (Acts 17:11).

Study Guide

— Chapter 1 —
The Disaster of Poor Communication

1. Give an example of a time when you were the victim of poor communication. What was the result?

2. Is there any price an unbeliever must pay in order to gain eternal life? Please explain and defend your answer biblically.

3. How does distinguishing eternal life from eternal rewards affect your understanding of assurance?

4. How is this distinction important for a clear communication of the gospel?

5. How does being properly motivated in your Christian service depend on understanding the difference between eternal life and eternal rewards?

6. As a Christian, have you ever lacked assurance (the certain knowledge that because of faith in Jesus you have eternal life and could never lose it)? If so, how did you regain it? If not, what has helped you stay sure you are eternally secure?

7. If you doubt that you are secure based on God's promise alone, your object of assurance becomes yourself instead of Christ. How would this affect your relationship with Him?

8. What happens to your understanding of the rewards passages of the New Testament when you lose sight of the fact that the only thing God requires of you for eternal life is faith in His immutable promise?

— Chapter 2—

WAGES AREN'T GIFTS

1.   Does the term *gift* have multiple meanings?

2.   If eternal rewards are pay for work done, doesn't this cheapen the death of Christ on your behalf? Defend your answer.

3.   If you don't distinguish between earned rewards and the gift of eternal life, what are the potential practical difficulties in your life?

4.   Why do you think some pastors and theologians argue that all believers will have the same quality of life in the kingdom and that rewards are gifts, not payments for work performed?

5.   Which single verse or passage in the Bible stands out to you as a strong defense for rewards (*misthos*) being compensation for work done? Why?

6.   How does the possibility of the Lord rewarding you for your life of service make you feel? Does it encourage you? Motivate you? Or does it discourage you? Why does it make you feel this way?

7.   How does knowing that eternal life is free change the way you view the doctrine of eternal rewards? How are these truths intended to work together to encourage and motivate the Body of Christ?

8.   Paul wrote Second Timothy just before his execution; thus, it is a very personal view of his heart. Read 2 Timothy 4:6-8. How did Paul understand and respond to the motivation of eternal rewards? What does this mean to you?

— Chapter 3 —

WE REALLY DO REAP WHAT WE SOW
Galatians 6:6-10

1. Why is the principle of sowing and reaping hard for some to believe?

2. Discuss how the analogy of sowing and reaping ties in with the point Paul is making in Galatians 6:6-10.

3. Compare verses 6 and 10. How are they similar and how are they different?

4. In light of Galatians 5, what specifically is sowing to the flesh? Is it, for example, willful rebellion against God as in the case of the Prodigal Son in Luke 15? Defend your answer.

5. Again, in light of Galatians 5, what specifically is meant by sowing to the Spirit?

6. Explain the difference between *possessing* eternal life and *reaping* eternal life.

7. How can eternal life be a free gift received by faith alone (John 4:10; 5:24; 6:47) and also be wages earned for work done (Galatians 6:7-9)? Why isn't this a contradiction?

8. How do you avoid losing heart in your Christian life?

— Chapter 4 —

FAITHFUL SERVANTS
Luke 19:11-27

1. Compare Luke 19:17 and 19:19. Discuss the similarities and differences between the Lord's response to each servant.

2. Defend the view that the third servant represents an unbeliever.

3. Defend the view that the third servant represents a third type of believer.

4. Who are the enemies of Jesus in this parable and what does their slaying in verse 27 signify?

5. How is Luke 19:11-27 similar to and different from Matthew 25:14-30?

6. Explain Luke 19:21-22. Does God really reap what He didn't sow? What is going on here?

7. What does putting money in the bank illustrate (Luke 19:23)? How could you do that today in a spiritual sense?

8. What does this passage have to say about those who persevere less than wholeheartedly in their service for Christ?

— Chapter 5 —
LOVING DISCIPLES
1 John 2:28; 4:17-19

1. Fear often has an object. You may fear stock market decline, loss of job or health, accidents, terrorist attacks, failure, etc. What is the specific object of fear in 1 John 4:17-19?

2. Are you afraid of "the day of judgment" (1 John 4:17)? Why or why not?

3. What precisely is "perfect love"?

4. Describe a time in your life when you felt confident (had boldness) and one in which you experienced shame. Compare those experiences to 1 John 2:28.

5. If your parents often mistreated you and were unfair with you, how might this affect the way you think about the Bema? If a person has an unhealthy attitude toward the Bema, how might he or she correct that attitude?

6. Give three or more examples in which someone you know showed "perfect love" toward you. How do you think their lives were enhanced by helping you?

7. Do you often reflect on the return of Christ? Do you think it is good to do? Why or why not?

8. What does it mean to "live today in light of eternity"?

— Chapter 6 —
NIKE CHRISTIANS
2 Timothy 2:11-13

1. What does Paul mean when he speaks of a believer dying with Christ? In what sense have Christians died with Him?

2. Why does Paul speak of living with Christ as future ("we shall also live with Him")? Don't believers already live with Christ?

3. In 2 Timothy 2:12a, what is entailed in the concept of endurance?

4. What does "denying Him" mean (2:12b)? Is this a one-time act, something that characterizes one's life, or how one is when his life ends (in death or the Rapture)? Can a born again person deny Christ in this sense?

5. What does Paul mean when he speaks of the Lord Jesus denying those who deny Him?

6. Explain 2 Timothy 2:13.

7. Explain how you think the following three people will fare at the Bema. (Hint: compare these people to 2 Timothy 2:11-13 and Luke 8:11-15 and Luke 19:11-26.)

a) Joe served Christ faithfully for thirty years and then drifted away from the Lord. He stopped going to church and no longer confessed His faith in Christ. For the last five years of his life he lives as a secret disciple.

b) Mary came to faith and began to grow spiritually. But within a year, she drifted away from the Lord. She lived the next forty years of her life as though God didn't exist. Then after the death of her husband, she returned to fellowship with the Lord.

For the last decade of her life she was a growing disciple who openly confessed Christ.

c) Shawn came to faith and served Christ halfheartedly his whole adult life. He failed to realize his potential as a Christian. Yet he endured in fellowship with Christ and in confessing Him.

8. Explain Matthew 10:32-33 in light of 2 Timothy 2:11-13.

— Chapter 7 —
CROSS BEARERS
Matthew 16:24-28

1. List the four uses of the Greek word *psychē* in Matthew 16:24-28.

2. What does losing one's *psychē* refer to in this context?

3. What does gaining one's *psychē* refer to in this context?

4. How was it possible for the disciples to have eternal life prior to the cross?

5. The Greek word *psychē* is used to speak of the Lord Jesus laying down His *life* for us (Matthew 20:28; Mark 10:45; John 10:11, 15, 17). Compare 1 John 3:16-18 and discuss how His laying down His *psychē* should impact your life.

6. What event preceded the Lord's comments in Matthew 16:24-28? How does keeping the context in mind help you understand these verses?

7. If you could gain the entire world, in terms of money, power, and fame, but you had to forfeit treasure, power, and fame in the life to come, would you do it? Would you be tempted to do it? Why or why not?

8. Does "each" in verse 27 refer to each *believer*? Or does it refer to each and every *person* who has ever lived, including all unbelievers? Defend your answer.

— Chapter 8 —
HUMBLE FOLLOWERS
Luke 17:7-10

1. How does Luke 17:5-6 serve as a transition between verses 1-4 and 7-10?

2. In verse 9, does the Lord mean that He will not thank us for our service? Why or why not?

3. What should your attitude be when you work hard and accomplish something while serving the Lord (verse 10)?

4. How does verse 10 apply to the Christian who is not working hard and serving the Lord?

5. Tell about a time that you observed another Christian exemplify a servant's heart. How did this impact you?

6. Compare Luke 17:7-10 with Matthew 23:11 and John 13:4-11.

7. Do you feel a sense of duty in your service for Christ? Why or why not? How can you cultivate a greater sense of duty?

8. Since God has chosen to obligate Himself to reward believers for their service, might there be a danger that we lose a sense of gratitude and develop an entitlement mentality? How can we avoid having such an attitude?

— Chapter 9 —
HEAVENLY TREASURE
Matthew 6:19-21

1. Write a brief account of someone you know who made significant personal sacrifice in the service of Christ.

2. Is saving for retirement an example of laying up treasure on earth? How about saving enough money for a down payment on a house? Owning a new car? How do you decide when you cross the line from prudent use of the money God has given you to laying up treasure on earth?

3. What does it mean to lay up treasures in heaven? Give concrete examples of how you can do that.

4. Using Revelation 21:24, build a case for the existence of an economy in the eternal kingdom.

5. In what way is heavenly treasure different from treasure on earth?

6. Where will treasure in heaven be enjoyed? Be careful, this *is* a trick question!

7. What does the Lord mean when He says, "Where your treasure is, there your heart will be also"?

8. In what way is heavenly treasure different from all other eternal rewards?

— Chapter 10 —
RULING WITH CHRIST

1. What are *active* and *passive* inheritances, and what is the biblical justification for these concepts?

2. Name ten different types of rulers in the nation of Israel. You might skim through 1–2 Samuel, 1–2 Kings, or 1–2 Chronicles for ideas.

3. Why would it be desirable to rule with Christ? After all, doesn't rulership entail a lot of hassles?

4. Do you want to rule with Christ? Why or why not?

5. Do you think that there would be a sense of regret for those believers who do not rule with Christ? Why or why not?

6. Consider the halfhearted Christian who will rule with Christ, but with only half the influence he could have had (Luke 19:19, compared with 19:17). Do you think that such a person will have a sense of regret?

7. The twelve disciples wanted to rule with Christ. Was this a good or a bad thing, they desired? Defend your answer.

8. Does the concept of being one of Christ's *partners* (*metachoi*) in the life to come evoke different feelings in you than the anticipation of being a *co-ruler* with Him? Why or why not?

— Chapter 11 —
SPECIAL PRIVILEGES

1. Do you think the prospect of earning special privileges is a proper way to motivate people to do their best? Why or why not?

2. Name the three most significant special privileges you ever earned in your family, school, work, or in other areas of life.

3. Why would entering the New Jerusalem by its gates be a privilege worth having?

4. What is the biblical significance of having a stone engraved with some special name that the Lord Jesus has given you?

5. Why would special foods like manna and the fruits of the tree of life be something worth having?

6. Do you find that the prospect of wearing special garments motivates you to serve Christ? Why or why not?

7. How does gaining these special privileges relate to the abundance of life referred to in John 10:10?

8. Explain the significance of ordinary things, such as your name, food, and clothing, being transformed into extraordinary privileges in the life to come. How does this highlight God's love for you?

— Chapter 12 —
HIS APPROVAL

1. What is approval?

2. What is the difference between approval and acceptance? How does the distinction help you to understand eternal rewards?

3. What was your initial reaction to the idea that the Lord Jesus will not approve of every believer when He judges us at the Bema?

4. What does gaining the approval of the Lord Jesus mean to you? How should it impact your daily living?

5. Will believers experience varying degrees of approval? What does this mean to you practically? Does this motivate you?

6. If a person walks with Christ faithfully for fifty years, then falls away, ceasing to go to church, pray, read the Bible, and confess Him, would he be approved due to his fifty years of service, or disapproved because of ending his life away from the Lord? Does the Bible speak on this? What does it say?

7. Do you think that the concept of approval as an eternal reward, distinct from eternal salvation, might be a helpful one to share with unbelievers? Why or why not?

8. How does the nature of this reward (His approval) help you to realize that, even in rewards, Christ is the focus, instead of yourself or the reward itself? Does this make you appreciate Him more?

— Chapter 13 —
FULLNESS FOREVER

1. Does Revelation 4:9-10 teach that you will give back whatever rewards you receive at the Bema? Defend your answer from this passage and from other New Testament verses.

2. Do you agree or disagree that the Millennium is the first 1,000 years of the eternal kingdom?

3. Do you agree or disagree that all eternal rewards last for one thousand years only? Defend your answer.

4. Would it motivate you more to strive for rewards if you knew they lasted forever and not simply for 1,000 years? Why or why not?

5. Pick out a few verses in Revelation 21–22 which suggest that some will rule with Christ in the eternal kingdom.

6. Do you agree or disagree with the suggestion that Matthew 6:19-21 shows that treasure stored in heaven will be everlasting? Why?

7. Do you see any comparisons and/or contrasts between working for many years for a nice retirement and working for Christ for many years so you can have a nice eternity? List some similarities and differences.

8. How does the eternal nature of these rewards magnify the Rewarder and humble the servant?

— Chapter 14 —
PREPARE TO MEET THE JUDGE
James 5:9

1. Do you normally think of the Lord Jesus as your Judge? How should His office of Judge affect your perception of Him and your service toward Him?

2. James was probably written within a year of the resurrection, yet believers in the church were already becoming weary of waiting for Christ's return. What does that say about our need to stay focused on Christ's impending return?

3. Compare James 5:9 with Revelation 3:20.

4. In light of James 5:9 and 1 John 1:9, will sins you confess still be judged at the Bema? Why or why not?

5. Does judgment according to works contradict justification by faith alone? Why or why not?

6. John 5:24 says that believers will not come into judgment. Harmonize that passage with James 5:9.

7. What is the door that is referred to in James 5:9? How does this highlight the expectancy of His coming? What does this mean for your relationship with Him?

8. Should you be concerned with His office as Judge, even though He is merciful? How does the Bible express the idea of His coming judgment of believers? Are you really held to a standard?

— Chapter 15 —
Remember Your Inheritance
Galatians 5:19-21

1. Have you ever inherited anything in which the amount you received reflected your treatment of the deceased? Or, do you know someone who had that experience? Explain what happened.

2. How do you know that Paul isn't saying that good works are required to keep eternal life?

3. Is Paul teaching that those whose lives are characterized by the deeds of flesh are not true believers?

4. Compare Ephesians 2:8-9 with Galatians 5:19-21, paying special attention to the verb tenses.

5. How is 2 Timothy 2:12 related to Galatians 5:19-21?

6. Explain the concepts of being an "heir of God" and a "joint heir with Christ" as found in Romans 8:17. How does this impact you?

7. Look over the list of sins in Galatians 5:19-21. Note some that don't seem to be as bad as others. Why do you think Paul includes seemingly lesser sins in this list?

8. What do the words "those who practice such things" in Galatians 5:21 mean? Is Paul thinking of what characterizes one's life? Of willful rebellion, unconfessed sins, or what?

— Chapter 16 —
WALK WITHOUT STUMBLING
Jude 24

1. Do a brief concordance study of Demas. Who was he and what happened to him?

2. Compare Jude 24 with 1 Corinthians 9:24-27.

3. Discuss the New Testament concept of being faultless. Is being faultless synonymous with being a believer? What are the implications of this?

4. What must a Christian do in order for God to keep him from stumbling?

5. When someone categorizes passages like Jude 24 as unconditional promises, what kind of attitude does this create?

6. On the other hand, what kind of attitude comes from knowing that God "is able to keep you from stumbling" if you trust Him to do so?

7. How does this apply to the Christian who has fallen?

8. What does it mean to be "before the presence of His glory with exceeding joy"?

— Chapter 17 —
KEEP YOUR EYES ON THE PRIZE
1 Corinthians 9:24-27

1. In what ways is the Christian life like a race?

2. What do crowns signify? Do you think Paul is thinking of literal crowns, literal crowns plus something else, or merely what the crowns symbolize? Defend your answer.

3. Contrast an *imperishable* crown with a *perishable* one.

4. How can you run with certainty in your Christian life?

5. Why does a Christian need to discipline his body?

6. How can a Christian discipline his body?

7. Discuss the New Testament concept of approval (*dokimos*).

8. How does the story of Alfred Rascon relate to your life? When you feel like you've been shot twice, blown up by a grenade, and shot again, are you going to fight on? Are you going to act in self-sacrificing love as he did? How will knowing that the Lord will reward you abundantly with an "imperishable crown" help you to do this?

– Scripture Index –

Luke

John

Acts

Romans

1 Corinthians

– Subject Index –

A Word About Grace Evangelical Society

Grace Evangelical Society (GES) was founded in 1986 by Dr. Bob Wilkin as an educational and motivational networking ministry. The purpose of GES is to promote the clear proclamation of God's free salvation and related, yet distinct, discipleship issues. GES accomplishes this purpose by the following means:

- a free bimonthly newsletter,
- a semiannual journal,
- commentaries on New Testament books,
- books by authors such as Zane Hodges, Earl Radmacher, Jody Dillow, and Bob Wilkin,
- audio tapes,
- conferences and seminars, and
- a non-resident seminary.

If you would like to receive our free newsletter or would like more information about the various ministries and publications listed above, you can contact us in any of the following ways:

- 972.257.1160 (phone),
- 972.255.3884 (fax),
- ges@faithalone.org (email),
- www.faithalone.org (website), or
- PO Box 155018, Irving, TX 75015-5018.

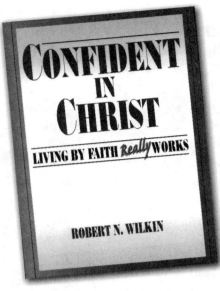